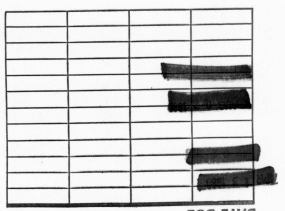

DATE DUE

HOPKINS' SANCTIFYING IMAGINATION

David Anthony Downes

UNIVERSITY
PRESS OF
AMERICA

LANHAM • NEW YORK • LONDON

Library of Congress Cataloging in Publication Data

Downes, David Anthony, 1927-
Hopkins' sanctifying imagination.

Bibliography: p.
Includes index.
1. Hopkins, Gerard Manley, 1844-1889—Criticism and
interpretation. 2. Christian poetry, English—History
and criticism. 3. Romanticism—England. I. Title.
PR4803.H44Z622 1985   821'.8   85-11071
ISBN 0-8191-4755-9 (alk. paper)
ISBN 0-8191-4756-7 (pbk. : alk. paper)

I dedicate this essay to Professor Norman H. MacKenzie to honor his distinguished contributions to Hopkins scholarship: "A perfect critic is very rare."

HOPKINS' SANCTIFYING IMAGINATION

I

In a rich notebook entry for the spring of 1871, Hopkins wrote of the films given off by his Lenten chocolate, candle smoke, and clouds. After setting down his penetrating observations, he remarked: "When you look hard at nature it seems to look hard at you, hence the true and the false instress of nature." He followed his comment with an illustration about streamers rising from Kemble End to demonstrate how nature can be falsely "instressed" if one does not let nature "look hard at you": "Unless you refresh your mind from time to time you cannot always remember or believe how deep the inscape in things is" *(Papers,* 204-5). The deepest "inscape" in things is Divine Presence. Looking, remembering, and believing are all part of a creative process of receiving the mysteries of existing things, especially their deific character. Gerard Manley Hopkins wrote poetry which can best be described as a refreshment of the mind's "looks" into the "inscapes" of things to the depth of a prophetic insight—meeting God.

This process of fully receiving the experiences of Nature Hopkins called "instressing." By this he meant a perceptive readiness to be open to the "looks" of the "inscapes" of being as well as an imaginative energy through which to encode the primordial language of things. Such "instressing" involves, besides a refreshing of the mind, the production of statements or utterances containing words powerful enough to reach into the very center of human consciousness. Poetry produced by what Hopkins called "instressing" the mystery of things takes on a sacral character of inspiration and beatitude.

Such an advanced experiential understanding of the unity of all being in and through its Divine subsidy brings about a sense of personal holiness and reverence, an awareness, sometimes bright and other times dim, of beatific mystery, and an elevation of the spirit that is both comforting and fearsome. The creative process by which such a religio-poetic state is produced can be described as the

1

workings of the sensibility of grace, a spiritual enablement by which the whole consciousness is sanctified, that is, opened up to the "inscape" of God being expressed in and through the primordial language of the "inscapes" of everything. Such "instressing looks" are the acts of the sanctifying imagination. They are pre-cognitive ways of seeing, receiving, and uttering powerful religious meaning. The opening words of the first stanza of Hopkins' "The Wreck of the Deutschland" is perhaps one of the grandest examples in all religious poetry: "Thou mastering me / God! giver of breath and bread; / World's strand, sway of the sea; / Lord of living and dead."

This essay is about the sanctifying imagination as it manifested itself in Hopkins' poetic art. Hopkins himself described the actions of the sanctifying imagination in stanza five of "The Wreck" where he wrote of the Divine presence in his own religious experience: "His mystery must be instressed, stressed; / For I greet him the days I meet him, and bless when I understand." "Instressing" the felt Divine Presence, meeting and greeting God in the very thicket of personal experience, these are the very elements of the sanctifying imagination operating in Hopkins' poetry. Hopkins wrote poetry to sanctify himself and others who were his readers. To this end he filled his poems with the richest sensibilities of grace, leaving, as we know, to heaven the religious and artistic destiny of his poetic art.

I start first with a brief recapitulation of the "higher" tradition of the English Romantics which was Hopkins' artistic heritage. This summary is followed by a tracing out of Hopkins' adaptations of this tradition through the theological mediations of John Henry Newman and the philosophic spirit of John Duns Scotus. Finally I turn my attentions to some of the esthetic and religious patterns of the sanctifying imagination revealed in Hopkins' mature poetry. The critical efforts will, I believe, show forth the true nature of Hopkins' poetic art. In addition to a delineation of Hopkins' unique sanctifying imagination, I wish to place his art in the broader historico-critical context of his literary culture, namely Romanticism, for the sensibility of grace about which I write was reawakened by the English Romantics who

2

revivified the sanctifying imagination at the beginning of the nineteenth century. I will try to show how Hopkins carried on the "higher" Romanticism of Wordsworth and Coleridge. The visionary levels of spiritual consciousness in the translucent poetry of these two great English Romantics are regenerated in the poetry of Hopkins. Indeed Hopkins was a member of that unique poetic group Harold Bloom has called "the visionary company," for his poetry is a "look" into the places where God dwells.

II

The first query which must be made about Hopkins' imagination concerns its Romantic ancestry. Critics have identified John Keats as the main creative influence on Hopkins largely because of the similarity of their esthetic sensibilities. Both produced some poetry full of imagery which might be described as having a similar hothouse lushness. However Keats was not the original shaping force of Hopkins' imagination. Wordsworth, Coleridge, and Newman provided the key notions out of which Hopkins developed his own concepts of poetic art and the uses of Christian Romanticism—one of the essential interests of this essay.

Scholars have traced out the basic religious elements of the Romantic imagination in numerous studies of the first generation of English Romantics./1/ In order to perceive where Hopkins began to build his own esthetic philosophic views and artistic practice, let us now sketch out the touchstones of religious Romanticism as students of Wordsworth and Coleridge have uncovered them. Then we will take a look at the way that John Henry Newman amalgamated Romantic religion with Christianity.

Wordsworth did not begin the effort to find an imaginative mode of language to account for "having seen something whatever that really was," as Hopkins noted; transcendent visionary experience has had a history from Plato to Blake./2/ In Wordsworth's case, as Stephen Prickett has shown in his work on Romantic religion, the sanctifying imagination took the form of attempting to

3

express deep, personal crises of a spiritual character through finding an artistic equivalent for the "language of Nature," the source of his intellectual and emotional stability. Wordsworth's imagination led him through some very sublime religious experiences (for example, the ascent of Snowdon episode in Book XIV of the *The Prelude)* to achieve some degree of wholeness in his life ("a blast of harmony") and in all life ("a chorus of infinity"). He experienced a kind of sanctifying, imaginative understanding in discovering himself to be part of some universal order in Nature superintending the ordinary world which appears to be so hopelessly divided. What produced Wordsworth's "inward agitations" was that he discovered a theological center in his deep love and reverence for Nature: "Wordsworth, in his poetry, exemplifies the spontaneous overflow of immanence into its opposite—transcendence."/3/ Transcendence is exactly the center of Hopkins' sympathetic reading of Wordsworth's "Immortality" ode; he felt the powerful pull of real spiritual crisis transformed into some vision of salvific unity. He wrote to R.W. Dixon, "human nature got another one of those shakes, and the tremble from it is spreading. This opinion I do strongly share; I am, ever since I knew the ode, in that tremble."/4/

What Wordsworth really raised was the question of how the language of Nature becomes the language of religion, the main subject of Coleridge's entire career. Coleridge searched deeply and diligently for some understanding of how the truths of Christianity, which he believed to be eternal, are expressed by the rational soul. Specifically he studied how scriptural narrative revelations of God can be harmonized with human language, the source of narrative revelations of human experience. Human language ordinarily is built out of generalities derived from discovering the lowest common denominator in variegated experience; however, divine Revelation is a wholly different form of utterance, as Coleridge explained: "[Biblical narratives] are the living *educts* of the Imagination; of that reconciling and mediatory power, which incorporating the Reason in Images of the Sense, and organizing (as it were) the flux of Senses by the permanence and self-circling energies of Reason, gives birth to a system of symbols, harmonious in

4

themselves, and consubstantial with the truths, of which they are the *conductors* . . . [thus] the Sacred Book is worthily intitled *the* WORD OF GOD."/5/

What Coleridge is saying is that the Bible is written in a special mode of language which functions at two levels and perspectives, thus at two depths. At the eternal level scripture narrates stories about God, His Presence, Power, and Paternity; and at the temporal level scripture reveals how God appears through religious experience in human history. Biblical language is a bi-valent system of signs which "by being particular and concrete . . . are symbolic of universal truths. . . . The fact that a person or an event is symbolic of wider truths does not detract from, but enhances its reality as particular and unique."/6/ The important note here is that Coleridge's idea of symbol is not the product of intellection as a form of generalization; rather such symbols are essentially forms of art expressive of the creative imagination functioning at its highest level—conductors of the Word. The symbols that such creative power produces possess a translucence whereby a particular experience is correlated to some more universal meaning.

For Coleridge the imagination is the most powerful and wonderful human faculty. The imagination is really the creator of a penetrating symbol-lens through which the sense-data of the objective world are discovered to be a living part of a higher reality, and in so doing, the symbol itself, catching both the sense particular and its eternal correlative, becomes a living, vital part of the unity of all Being it renders more fully intelligible. Coleridge stressed again and again this bi-polarity of the symbolic expressive powers of the imagination, as Prickett observes: "Thus over and over again we find Coleridge describing the 'Imagination' in terms of bringing into a single focus two separate levels of experience, and seeing them as a coherent whole. His concept of the Imagination is essentially 'stereoscopic'; it stands at the intersection of two different perspectives and so enables us to see 'in depth.' "/7/

Scriptural narratives are the "living *educts* of the Imagination," then, because they possess so powerfully the bi-polarity of "at once Portraits and Ideals." Thus reading the Bible impresses upon the reader this stereoscopic function of its language—its outer, historical dimension narrating the lives of the prophets, saints, Christ Himself; and the inner, personal assent of the reader being sanctified. The symbol of the "Logos" is a perfect example of Coleridge's "stereoscopic" imagination: in its outer meaning there is revealed Person (Incarnation), sacred history (Creation and Redemption), and the Word (Second Person of the Trinity). The soul is opened up to the mystery of Divinity as transcendental "otherness" standing in judgment of the world, an omnipotent Presence viewed as above and within time, history, Nature, and human personality. This co-Presence, as Stephen Prickett notes, is "the unresolvable tension between the world of things—what Coleridge called 'It is'—and the world of our intuitive moral awareness—what Coleridge called 'I am.' "/8/ The imagination is the power by which we "understand" this tension, and the language produced is primarily a religious language which is the unifying symbol system bringing language itself to its fullest creative, expressive powers, its "LIVING POWERS," as Coleridge put it. The distinguishing characteristic of this language is its capacity for "transcendental" meaning, its poetic power to point beyond itself and in that pointing to become transfigured in meaning beyond what is. Poetic language of this quality can be understood only in terms of its transcendental symbolic complexity. Wordsworth's language of Nature and Coleridge's language of religion are the very constitutive elements of Hopkins' poetic language, for Hopkins' poetry is the "spontaneous overflow of immanence" into transcendence accomplished through Christianity being the "living *educt* of the Imagination."

Hopkins became the poet Wordsworth and Coleridge described as the ideal poet. He used his imaginative powers to discover deeper religious implications in the structures of poetic language thereby producing a poetry whose form and meaning move beyond the esthetic to the prophetic mode of experience. The poetic continuity between Wordsworth, Coleridge, and Hopkins lies in this transformation of poetic language to become an expression of the sanctified consciousness, a multi-level state of spiritual apprehension

6

wherein God's Presence is affirmed in the prism of personal culture and experience. Following Wordsworth and Coleridge, no Romantic poet has demonstrated more clearly the unity of poetic and religious language than has Hopkins.

The Christian relevance of the Romantic imagination came to Hopkins, however, most immediately and directly through the general mentorship of John Henry Newman. Newman placed the heritage of Wordsworth and Coleridge into a framework of orthodox religious belief which touched Hopkins directly in his own experience of conversion and priestly vocation. We must see how Newman related the Romantic imagination and religious experience to the spiritual psychology of Christian assent.

That Newman felt a deep cultural kinship with Wordsworth has been well established./9/ The center of their relationship is a peculiarly sensitive childhood during which both apparently experienced very deep spiritual sensations about their surroundings. These deep feelings produced in each a powerful impulse to look at his life very intensely, with the result that each constructed out of personal experience a number of notions touching upon the profoundest questions of religion, philosophy, and art. In both the autobiographical impulse was the shaping force which established the touchstone of all of their thought and its expression, namely, that the validation of any truth involves the test of lived experiences—a "life test," the hallmark of English Romanticism. Newman, like Wordsworth, in attempting to understand any principle of truth always sought to examine his own act of perception of the direct experience of the issue as it came to him in his own life circumstances. This principle of "life test" analysis accounts for every serious work Newman wrote. His writings abound with references to his personal experiences.

But how can vital self-knowledge leading to true understanding be discerned among all the diversities of self-rationalization? In the long ensuing debate such a search involves (an extensive quest for the true Church of Christianity, for example) Newman applied the Wordsworthian impulse *to see* in one's own direct experience those vital signs of the organic consciousness which constitutes a living form of life. But how could he be sure of his own act of perception? How free was his perception from the mind's powerful ability to rationalize experience into its own terms and meaning? Newman's pursuit of this question led him directly to Coleridge's consideration of how we "see into the life of things."

The answer, as it had for Wordsworth and Coleridge, lay in discovering a single basic principle whose richness of application made life whole and unified. All three found that any integration between a living form of life and the experience of it could be accomplished only in terms of a religious principle, in Newman's case Catholic Christianity. Hence for Newman validation of the perception of experience was a question of how to account for religious consciousness and religious assent. To achieve an understanding of belief, Newman, like Wordsworth and Coleridge, found that the rationalist traditions of philosophic inquiry offered little help. He was left with applying his own "life test," like the understandings of Wordsworth and Coleridge, in the very substance of his own life.

Newman first began with himself in the best Wordsworthian manner. The result was the *Apologia Pro Vita Sua*, a most careful assessment of how he experienced that most profound of all "living forms," the process of assent to a religious understanding of life. His moving and powerful account is written in the language of "self-discovery" the creativity of which is to see the reality of the patterns of his religious consciousness. Careful analysis and accurate narration of his own conversion process as a series of perceptive acts could lay open the true relationship between life and faith. The story of the growth of the assenting religious consciousness that is the *Apologia* is uniquely Newmanesque, but its mode is applied Wordsworth.

However, the power of sensitive detachment and complete openness did not answer completely either Charles Kingsley's erroneous charge nor did it establish conceptually Newman's position on the differences between "notion" and "real assent" in the psychology of religious belief. Newman

8

himself understood this incompleteness in his explanation and meditated upon this key understanding over a long period of time. Finally he set down his position in a book he called *A Grammar of Assent* (see note 10). As is well known now, Newman argued that reason alone (notionality) cannot ground faith. A stronger force was necessary to establish and keep alive personal belief, what he called "real assent." Without going into Newman's dialectic in any detail, the character of which has been carefully assessed, let us see what he meant by "real assent." This summary will be sufficient to allow us to see the impact of Coleridge upon Newman's thinking.

In the Christian tradition of Paul and Augustine, Newman affirmed conceptually that two kinds of knowledge shape human consciousness. One is notional, the other real. Coleridge made a similar distinction calling these two states "passive" and "active" states of mind. Newman found in Coleridge a re-confirmation of his own position that any assent which penetrated one's whole being came from a *real* growth of mind. As for any true and real experience, religious experience, to be truly authentic, had to show signs of vitality. How can one perceive such growth of the religious consciousness? On this matter Newman followed Coleridge,/10/ agreeing that it is the imaginative faculty which makes translucent through its penetrating and symbolizing powers the living process of the life of faith.

Of course, Newman offered his own account of this creative process. Starting with Coleridge, he set out to describe more specifically how human consciousness takes in "concrete imaginatively realised fact" in contrast to the assimilation of facts that are "abstract and essentially unrealised." How then in the dialectic of these two knowledge processes does one move from a change of mind (notion) to the mind changing (real assent)? Newman argues in his *Grammar* that living growth in the mind is a process of "real ratiocination" produced by a "present imagination." This is to say that the imaginative process energizes the illative sense of the human mind "making the abstract concrete, the notional real. . . . The illative imagination is the principle which rightly interprets the riddle [the

9

doctrine of the Trinity, for example] ... and converts a chaos into an orderly and luminous whole."/11/ In this way experience comes to be understood as a part of the organicism of real life, possessing its own inner order of vitality and growth, and at the same time partaking in the holistic system of total being. As for Wordsworth and Coleridge, so for Newman, experience (our total sense world) is a "form of life" possessing inner and outer, linear and transcendental, unity. Christianity, Newman argues, as did Coleridge, is the deepest structure of a "form of life" at the level of the deepest structure of reality.

It is in the consideration of Catholic Christianity as a deep structure that Newman went beyond Coleridge. Led by the illative imagination penetrating religious experience, real assent grows to take in beliefs which receive our irrevocable assent; these assents lead us into living the Christian "form of life," for the active and alive illative imagination will discover its "living educts" in the narratives of the Holy Bible. The shaping forces of these assents upon our lives will incline toward the communal expression of Christian living even though retaining their highly personal and individual character. Sometimes, however, a genuine tension arises between private belief and communal confirmation. What, then, keeps private belief pure and how is its purity validated in human society? Precisely at this juncture Newman went beyond Coleridge, as Stephen Prickett observes:

> The creative power of the illative imagination leaps boldly from inference and probability to certainty, as if thinking God's thoughts after him. The key difference from Coleridge lies in that word "rightly." For Coleridge the bi-focal symbolizing power of the imagination had always seemed to carry with it some kind of self-authenticating guarantee of truth. For Newman, this was plainly not so in all cases. The problem of truth or falsity of the imagination was one that became very important to him. Though he himself seems

10

to come very near to Coleridge's assumption of self-authentication in the *Essay on the Development of Christian Doctrine,* the guarantee is in fact given here not by the symbolizing process itself (as it often appears to be with Coleridge) but by the special subject-matter: an infallibly guided Church. To interpret rightly is not a gift of the illative imagination working by itself. .../12/

Newman, then, affirmed that real assent must be safe-guarded by a Divinely sanctioned form of life which, through its own vitality, its own organic living process, is kept permanently in touch with the highest, and only source of religious truth—the Holy Spirit. Here lies Newman's uniqueness, as Prickett notes: "Newman had developed the Romantic theological tradition of Wordsworth and Coleridge with sensitivity, skill, and brilliant reasoning. He is the theological climax of the fiduciary tradition. There is a ratiocinative power in his writing that Coleridge and Wordsworth, for all their insights, never possessed."/13/

What has been briefly summarized is the Romantic theological tradition that Hopkins inherited, a tradition about which he was very conscious. His approach to Nature was through Wordsworth's language of Nature. No Romantic poet was more dedicated to the authentication of direct sense experience by dwelling upon the way individual perception connected human consciousness and the forms of Nature. Hopkins understood Wordsworth's "shocks" and he too was put into a "tremble." Like Wordsworth, Hopkins affirmed that the perceptual journey into Nature is a journey of self-discovery. Stephen Prickett rightly suggests that Hopkins at twenty-one may be claimed "as Wordsworth's true successor as a 'nature poet' in the nineteenth century. . . ."/14/

In Coleridge Hopkins found the very model of his own Imagination. Though he was to develop his own philosophical explanation on the matter, he began with Coleridge. For Hopkins, as well, the imagination possessed special

11

powers of perception in a world in which "Ideals" and "Portraits" had to be discerned. The task of the imagination is to show how these two polarities under the tension of opposing principles of being are reconciled in the translucence of symbolic statements which light up the immanence of the Holy and Eternal lodged in the datum of individual experience. Like Coleridge, Hopkins used the imagination to produce a poetry of reconciliation, and like Coleridge, the sources of imaginative power were the "living educts" of Scripture. The imagination, full of creative light, can *see* the wholeness of Creation in one of its particulars and can *capture* that luminous sight in a carol of celebrating consent. As the imagination opens up the world, it opens up the soul to the special bond underlying the world—the mystery of sacral sublimity and sinful ignobility. *The Ancient Mariner* and "The Wreck of the Deutschland" are grand parallel instances of how the imagination produces this awesome reconciliation.

Newman, of course, was Hopkins' direct mentor. He validated for Hopkins how God was so personally present in his own direct experience and the need to affirm that Presence both in his own life and in some authenticated communal way. Hopkins understood the workings of Newman's illative imagination in his own conversion to Catholicism and his vocation to the priesthood. As for Coleridge and Newman, so for Hopkins; Christianity is a "form of life" thriving on every level of existence. This mystery is the meaning of the Incarnation which is the major focus of all of Hopkins' writing.

Hopkins developed his own philosophy of art and religion out of this Romantic theological framework. He, of course, set down his own conceptual account of these subjects as he did live them as a poet and a priest. We are now ready to trace the development of Hopkins' stereoscopic Romantic imagination plumbing direct experience, exercising its illative sense to become the sanctifying imagination.

Before beginning this effort, I wish to remind the reader of what I said at the outset of this essay regarding Hopkins' place in the Romantic tradition. It is the burden of my argument that Hopkins' understanding and use of his Christian Romantic imagination was to develop a sanctifying art and that this is the special character of his poetry. If this be true, Hopkins was a true Romantic in the sense of that term that pervades the writings of Harold Bloom and F. X. Shea. Like them, I understand Romanticism as essentially a state of religio-artistic consciousness, that its gospel is poetry, that its mentality comprises a metaphysic, a theory of history, and that Romanticism is a luminescent state of soul vision having the greatest implications for living the fullest human life. In the wake of Milton's notion of Christian liberty, Bloom stresses the Protestant dissenting background in the formation of the Romantic consciousness that made up the "visionary company" of the first two generations of English Romantics./15/ He places no Victorian poet in that membership and, indeed, considers only W. B. Yeats and Wallace Stevens as true inheritors. In this essay, I attempt to place G. M. Hopkins in this "visionary company" because he converted his Catholic Christianity to the awakened spirit of the Romantic seer in his poetry. Most scholarship has studied Hopkins as priest-poet, or Catholic-Christian. I read Hopkins as an authentic high Romantic, a true inheritor of Milton, Wordsworth, and Coleridge, and the only Victorian "high Romantic" ancestor to Yeats and Stevens.

III

Hopkins very early in life found himself drawn strongly and deeply to both the cognitive and Romantic impulses in his own nature. For instance, he was very attracted to that aspect of his religious experience which generated creative energies. His notebooks, letters, and poems all exemplify this. At the same time, his intellectual powers caused him to approach religion in categorical ways. The result was a tension in him which can be seen even in his early poetry as a cross-purpose between declaring religious experience and merely witnessing. "The Escorial," while a youthful poem, nevertheless is an instance of the declaring spirit in the sense that the poem is a precocious demonstration of putting religious history into verse, and while the poetic declarations indicate an advanced esthetic awareness, the

13

poet is not expressing assimilated direct, personal experience. Instead we have abstractive poetic statements about the historical religious heritage of the Escorial:

> . . . the Escorial
> Arose in gloom, a solemn mockery
> Of those gilt webs that languish'd in a fall.
> This to remotest ages was to be
> The pride of faith, and home of sternest
>   piety./16/

This passage, and most of the rest of the poem, is mainly a notable studio piece. Critics like John Robinson and Elisabeth Schneider/17/ have seen in the passages wherein Hopkins offers some very descriptive lines of St. Lawrence's martyrdom a possible indication of a direct reflection of Hopkins' religious sensibility in action, but this is doubtful. Lines like "For that staunch saint still prais'd his Master's name / While his cracked flesh lay hissing on the grate"/18/ strike me as a good example of a conventional poetic statement in which there is no sign of any true feeling arising from experience and therefore no indication of any real involvement on the part of the poet.

A perusal of the remainder of the early religious poems reveals a gradual loosening of the modeling impulse, but the declarative poetic generalization often still predominates. In his early religious poetry, however, there are those passages in which the poet is in earnest to capture some imaginative distillation of his true religious feelings. Therefore, while we still get many lines like, "An so my trust, confused, struck and shook / Yields to the sultry siege of melancholy,"/19/ we also find his lovely poem, "The Habit of Perfection": "Elected silence, sing to me / And beat upon my whorled ear, / Pipe me to pastures still and be / The music that I care to hear."/20/ Hopkins' early poetry remains a practicing of the scales from which the true music would come. But the integrity of deepening reverence in these early poems presaged religious poetry of great power. Already Hopkins' religious experience was beginning to be penetrated by his Romantic visionary imagination.

14

To find how direct experience began to be shaped by Hopkins' Romantic sensibility, readers must turn to his *Notebooks*. Here Hopkins' growing imaginative powers played with sights, sounds, images, and words. Entry by entry, these passages record the very roots and soil of his Romantic spirit. Read alongside the poetry of the same period, we discover the other Hopkins, the Romantic teasing his creative awareness this way and that, always fascinated by the many ways perception shapes response, how image breeds words, and words cluster into a song of words, "Grind, gride, gird, grit, grate, graet. . . ."/21/ The early poetry and the notebooks taken together show forth developing rationalist and Romantic tendencies in Hopkins' creative personality. Both expressions in these writings make clear the presence of a dynamic tension in his nature out of which he would generate some great prose and poetry.

I believe that Hopkins' intellectual impulses energized by his strong Romantic feelings give us perspective on his conversion to Catholicism and his becoming a Jesuit. His drive for the deepest intensity of religious experience throughout his life always had a conceptual side. All his life Hopkins expressed a desire to attain the utmost purity of consciousness in some form of defined standards and ideals. The character of this moral scaling was always to some degree Evangelical Protestant, which is to say, he felt an abiding discomfort with the denseness of direct experience and a need for a moral exactness. His powerful Romantic engagement with immediate sensibility caused him to try to choose some hard disciplinary way to traduce experience or transform it. To the Protestant Evangelical consciousness, experience is often an untrustworthy vessel of truth; only the inscrutable will of God, mysterious and otherworldly, expresses true reality. All his life Hopkins had to contend with this Protestant either/or pattern in his personality, which in his case leaned heavily to scrupulosity and thus to exaggeration. No wonder that the poet in him felt hounded and neglected. He later explained that it was because of his Jesuit priesthood that he locked up the Romantic poet in him, but, of course, brilliance with priestly integrity has never been incompatible with the

Catholic priesthood, especially among the Jesuits. The more likely truth is that Hopkins' Protestant categorical moral approaches to religious experience caused him to seek exact measures of spiritual commitment.

Indeed, Hopkins' conversion to Catholicism had its Protestant side. Questions about the Apostolic Succession, doctrinal perseverance, and general Church discipline could be answered out of a long "rationalist" tradition of Catholic theology. While not discounting a Romantic side of his conversion—Newman and hero worship, for example—still to a young classicist steeped in the Platonic spirit of pure rationalism, the "rationalist-Scholastic" tradition of Catholic theology must have proved very attractive. Would not Catholic intellectualism have been a religious equivalent to his intellectual patron, Plato? Plato attracted him, as he said in a school essay, because the Platonic genius was a unique "Intellectualism" which offered "opportunities for endless balancing, antithesis as well as parallel."/22/ His school essay really describes a great philosophic challenge Hopkins perceived in his own time, that of fusing several systems of thought and culture into some splendid order, a "new Realism," just as Plato had attempted a synthesis in Greek thought. This is a brave and bold aspiration for any young man, but there is no question Hopkins felt his powers up to the task.

Moreover, the Catholic Church spanned the universe of Western thought with a universality suitable to such aspirations. Catholic tradition in all of its longevity was not lost on young Hopkins, as he noted in his essay. There were, he said, deep divisions in Western philosophic systems which have come about since the Middle Ages and the Reformation. He wondered how "great thinkers" fit into developing Western intellectual and cultural history. Does Shakespeare represent the bouquet of the medieval world or the flowering of the English Renaissance? Was Wordsworth bringing the Enlightenment to its final fruition or was he expressing the planting of a new movement? Newman and the Oxford Movement raised pointedly the true place of Catholic culture in Western religious thought. In order to attempt a new intellectual synthesis, the Roman Church offered any aspiring new Platonist with a holistic bent an ancient wall of theological and philosophical tradition upon which to add and build. In his school essay on Plato and the Greek world, Hopkins saw a model: ". . . Plato was able to feel the sadness of complex thought running to different conclusions when the old unit of belief which gives meaning to every subordination of thought and action was gone."/23/ Perhaps Hopkins' tensions between his powerful philosophical ideals and his equally powerful Romantic engagement with direct experience are reflected in his comments about Plato's predicament: "Perhaps we may say that in raising the new religion of the Ideal Good to fill the place of the old we feel less his enthusiasm for the new truth, the One, the Good, or whatever it is called, than his despair at the multiplicity of phenomena unexplained and unconnected, and the pettiness of the poets on the side of the imagination."/24/ Opposite the passage "unexplained and unconnected," Hopkins wrote on a blank page, "unexplained and unconnected,—the heavy and weary weight of all this unintelligible world, the inconsistency, etc."

He pointed out that Plato's great contribution to Western thought was to confront the old thought system and to show the way to a new beneficial plan. Is this what faced contemporary thinkers in his own time? Hopkins perhaps saw in Plato his great challenge. An awesome task, yet Plato provided an exemplar in his own methodology: "But its use was to have shown how to apply searching intelligence to all kind of matter and to press on the attention the beginnings of many speculations on thought and its relations to outer things."/25/ Another way of saying this might be that Hopkins felt the intellectual need and the personal challenge to connect the visionary dream gifts of Romantic personality to some sound, abstract thought system like the philosophy of science. Somehow the great power of the affective consciousness might be unified with clear and distinct ideas in the rational consciousness.

However much Hopkins felt the weight of the "unexplained and unconnected" in his Victorian mind, he was not despairing. In another school essay, "The Probable Future of Metaphysics,"/26/ he put down the task for modern critical thinking. The problem? How to reconcile the quarrel between abstractionism (metaphysics) and experience (psychology). Other names for these two camps are rationalism (reason) and Romanticism (senses): "The tide we may foresee will always run and turn between idealism and materialism. . . ." He suggests that the nineteenth century is an "afternoon" age of experience following the "morning" of the absolutist mind. He assumes that such a movement has its intrinsic development, but whatever that is, he finds in his analysis of past Western thought, along with the more recent "great seasons in the history of philosophy," a clear necessity for a new great fusion of systems of thought, a "new Realism" in which the Platonic intellect is integrated with the imaginative reason of Romantic sensibility.

In this essay Hopkins speculates that the metaphysics of the future may well be the establishment of a metaphysical conception of an ordered "string" of being which the mind can grasp; and yet there will be some created forms in existence which the abstractionist mind will find inexplicable. Moreover, experience will always generate ideas, he argues, even though rationalism will maintain it is the other way around. Therefore Romanticism cannot be dismissed as an intellectual force. However, the Romantic personality with its great capacity to penetrate experience and recreate it in some expressive form will have to accept some principle of objective truth to proportion its deep sense of subjective veracity, to ground its insights in some conceptual system.

There is evidence in Hopkins' undergraduate essays of a youthful mind sprouting an amazing understanding of the central philosophic questions which confront the modern mind. These essays suggest in rough outline a line of inquiry leading to some synthesis of the forms generated by imaginative reason (by interacting with personal experience) and the ideas generated by the intellective reason (by abstracting theories from observed sense data). In Hopkins' own intellectual and artistic development, this synthesis took the form of correlating Romanticism (religion and poetry) and notionalism (faith and theology). His construction of this issue of theories versus Personality really states one of the most fundamental historical and religious questions in the Western world: Is the Incarnation the ultimate validation of reason and experience? I suggest that it is possible to understand Hopkins' life and work as a grappling with this profound issue in the guise of his own intellectual, moral, and artistic struggles. If this is true, then his becoming a Catholic and eventually a Jesuit makes sense on an entirely different level than personal belief. The Catholic Church offered him the kind of philosophic and theological tradition out of which he could ground his synthesis within a long and learned tradition, and provided him with the apposite career opportunities to pursue his artistic and intellectual aspirations. The Jesuits specifically possessed, more than any other society in the Catholic Church—so was its reputation —the most rigorous intellectual tradition, the most aggressive sense of the modern world, and the greatest power in the Roman Church. In these speculations I do not wish to understate the religious reasons Hopkins might have had for becoming a Catholic and a Jesuit; of course, he had religious reasons which were prime, but he also had intellectual and artistic ones, the greatest evidence for this dual motivation in him being his life-long struggle to find a fulfilling, personal realization as a Jesuit intellectual and a Jesuit poet. Hopkins' letters, papers, and notebooks strongly support these patterns in his career./27/

IV

The Romantic religious context of Hopkins' life and work is, I believe, a broader, more significant one than most scholars have taken in discussing Hopkins, wider than Protestant-Catholic, priest-poet, Victorian-Jesuit, all of which are subsumable under the more general conceptions I am suggesting. In the rest of this essay I wish to show the validity of such an approach by discussing some vital connections in Hopkins' career where his "new Realist" Romantic mind is in evidence. In the end, I am really arguing that Gerard Hopkins was a different kind of Catholic and Jesuit, a unique Victorian poet, and an extraordinary human being because of the shaping forces of his Romantic consciousness.

19

First, the Jesuit Catholic. It is important to remember that the person who became a Catholic and then a Jesuit priest had primarily a Romantic personality. Hopkins was, as his notebooks, drawings, and music make very clear, deeply engaged with seeing and experiencing the outer world and seriously involved in imaginatively exploring and expressing his own consciousness, intellectually and imaginatively, as a way of authenticating his visionary powers. At the same time, his Romantic imaginative intellect affirmed some universal component in his experience possessing some transcendent attributes before which he felt some profound assent. Only in this security could a Romantic personality like Hopkins' rescue experience from the constant atrophy of change and finitude. It is thus vital for experience to be anchored to some more permanent form beyond personal reality. The search for a sublime center in experience was a doubly dangerous pursuit risking rampant subjectivism on the one hand and selfless abstractionalism on the other.

That something like this Romantic psychology was on Hopkins' mind is evident from some notes he wrote on Greek philosophy in his *Notebooks*./28/ Briefly summarized, he wrote that every existent has an intrinsic energy which is conductable to all Being: ". . . Being is and Not-being is not. . . ." This Being energy is the way consciousness and the world meet, he believed, each entity touching the same power in the other, each contributing some form of energy in the contest, thus each confronting the other with an individualized expression of Being—energy. In the non-human external world, this energy is a basic existent-being energy; in the human order of conscious awareness this energy is a psycho-being energy as well. Hopkins created his own term for these notions of being energies in all things, his famous "instress." Since "instress" energies take individuated forms of conduction in all things, he created another term, "inscape," for the outward manifestation of this inner being-power in all things.

Using these two notions and terms, Hopkins formulated a theory of knowing. For him the apprehension of the visible world by a discerning consciousness involves the conduction of one stress to the other. This flow of being-power is always carried through the circuitry of "inscape," that is, "stress" is expressed as a "scape." Since every manifestation of basic being-power within all things ("instress") is expressed as an individualized mode ("inscape"), the very act of being this or that is a form of self-authentication. Put more simply, being is an affirmation of a being-power as this thing or that person. Hopkins put in his school essay, "But indeed I have often felt when I have been in the mood and felt the depth of an instress or how fast an inscape holds a thing, that nothing is so pregnant and straightforward to the truth as simple *yes* and *is*."/29/ With this formulation of the basic ontological character of existent being, Hopkins laid the groundwork for the Romantic-cognitive perceptual process. Experience involves direct encounter through "inscape" with intrinsic powers within things ("instress"). The conduction of this being-stress offers the possibility for a hookup between consciousness and all being. The main point of Hopkins' argument, of course, is that direct and immediate experience carries within it the potential for a higher awareness beyond experience, a hierarchy of purer forms of existence, ultimately the Universal Ideal. This extraordinary leap of consciousness Hopkins thought Wordsworth experienced and told of in his *Intimations* ode: ". . . human nature in these men saw something, got a shock . . . in a tremble ever since."

The multiplicity of variously complex forms of sensible existents suggests that there is an order of "inscapes," a hierarchy of grouping of "stress-Being." If this is so, then any individual self-expression of "stress" through the circuity of "scape" constitutes a form of authentication of individual selfness and, at the same time, an affirmation of all Being and/or whole classes of Being—"simple yes and is." So in knowing the One individually, the Many can be discerned in a more universal awareness. This is more than a restatement of the old classical One and Many solution. Hopkins asserted that the same basic Being-energy is in all Being at all levels, which explains the connection in real existence of the same Being-stress in each individual existent, each class of existents, and all existence. His solution was not one in which the "agent intellect" solved the problem as a mental logicality. The Being stress on the mind is the same that exists in all Being from the lowest to the highest orders. If this ontological principle be true, then experience (contact with any sensible being) can by "instressing" through the creative faculties of the imagination lead to higher and higher awareness of Universal Being. Univocal principles of Being throughout all existence explain how the basic milieu of Romantic consciousness—real and direct experience—can become a means of transport to a more transcendent awareness of an Ideal order of things, a transport which is accomplished by the "eyes" of the imagination seeing beyond the "inscape" of particulars to the ultimate "stress" of all existence. Hopkins here sketched out his version of the Incarnational imagination affirming the powers of the "Primary Imagination" following Coleridge./30/

This reconciliation of Personality with Being cannot be overemphasized in Hopkins. Later in his career when Hopkins was seeking ways in which to bring these earlier philosophic notions into the rationalist traditions of Catholic theology, he clearly rejected the standard anti-Romantic positions offered to him in the guise of the seminary theology of Francisco Suarez. Instead he chose Scotus as his scholastic guide to Catholic theology./31/ I submit the prime reason he did so was that Scotus affirmed Hopkins' own notion of the very same "stress" in all things as there is in God and the human imaginative-intuitive powers to obtain a "visio existentis." Through Scotus, Hopkins was able to bring his own philosophic solutions into the Catholic theological tradition. For example, in the Scholastic mode, he developed a new proof for the existence of God, "a Romantic proof," based upon "instress" and "inscape," by which the imaginative reason opened up a circuitry which conducted the individual consciousness through real experience to universal being—transcendent Divinity and immanent Deity—the Incarnation. Out of such theological insights, Hopkins built an understanding of how his religious experience, penetrated by the spiritualizing visionary Imagination, could catch Christ-God in the swoop or song of a bird.

Where and how do the imaginative powers of "wording" of poetry fit into Hopkins' Romantic-Christian explanation? He postulated that "knowing" must be a form of "stress." From this it follows "wording" must be a version of "stress" because words are "inscapes" of thinking. He wrote: "To be and to know or being and thought are the same. The truth in thought is Being, stress, and each word is one way of acknowledging Being and each sentence by its copula *is* (or its equivalent) the utterance and assertion of it." As in his philosophic solution, so in his poetic solution; the key idea is Hopkins' attribution of univocal Being to all existents. If the same Being in every finite thing is in infinite Being, then experience of the finite visible world can be a basis for coming into contact with the infinite and invisible; this is Hopkins' equivalent of Coleridge's Primary Imagination— ". . . the living power and prime agent of all human perception. . . ." Wording (or poetry) of such imaginative transport is rooted in the individual consciousness experiencing. The symbolizing Imagination, "stressing and instressing," is able to "inscape" in "wording" (symbols) the ascending consciousness in all of its richly personalized apprehension, revealing the "Translucence of the Eternal through and in the Temporal," as Coleridge put it. Penetrating experience to these higher levels of being constitutes for Hopkins, as it did for Wordsworth and Coleridge, the very essence of the uses of the religious imagination. Such a religious poem is a unique "inscape" of the experience of "instressing" Being to its mysterious source. Poetic language is transformed into a religious language rich with the felt intensity of the awe of a sublime journey of ascent from the ordinary datum of natural experience to the Holy Presence behind and beyond everything.

In these early writings, then, Hopkins sketched the outlines of what amounted to his own understanding of Romanticism and religion. He never developed a full statement of his mind on the subject. We are left to follow his hints as well as make them richer through later statements and practices. While the influence of Newman, Scotus, and St. Ignatius have been to some degree anticipated in this discussion of the early formative phases of Hopkins' Romantic formulations, more must be said about these more direct mentors.

Hopkins' first prolonged, direct, formal contact with Catholicism happened during his years at Newman's Oratory School where he was a teacher from September 1867 to April 1868. Hopkins went to the Oratory to ponder the implications of his becoming a Catholic and to determine his religious vocation. Little is known about the details of his conversion to Catholicism except that his mind had been permanently changed regarding his duty to become a Catholic. Newman's arguments in all of their illative powers probably led Hopkins to his decision. At least we know when he repeated his own arguments to Newman when they first met, they were in complete accord./32/

As for the influences upon Hopkins, later in his life, of Newman's formal account of the process of religious assent put forth in his *A Grammar of Assent,* we can only conjecture. We know that though the book was published in 1870, Hopkins did not read it until three years later. He said he admired in Newman's more reasoned statement his "justice and candour and gravity and rightness of mind," but had less satisfaction over its style./33/ He read the *Grammar* during his years as a Scholastic studying at the Jesuit house at St. Mary's Hill, Stonyhurst, where he was being introduced to the Scholastic tradition of medieval philosophy; also at this time Scotus came to his attention. Between traditional Catholic philosophy, Newman, and Scotus, we know he chose Scotus as his philosophic mentor to go along with Ignatius as his spiritual guide. This did not mean that Newman's mentality, his *Grammar,* had no continual sway on his mind. Indeed, Hopkins offered to Newman to do a commentary on his book, most likely from a Scotistic Scholastic point of view, but Newman demurred./34/ Fr. Christopher Devlin suggests that Hopkins possessed some conjectures about an equivalent to Newman's key notions in the *Grammar* of "notional" and "real" assent might be found in *The Spiritual Exercises* where Ignatius speaks of *intima cognitio* and Scotus' idea of practical knowledge./35/

Moreover Hopkins was hoping to bring these three great mentors into some intelligible relationship. This desire would be built on his real knowledge of the effects of these three great spirits upon his own life. Of the three Newman received least cogitation, but this is understandable, for Newman's illative imagination had been fully operative in Hopkins, the poet. Again and again the poems demonstrate the true character of real assent. Hopkin's abstractive mind was shaped primarily by Scotistic Scholastic principles, but his poetry has the strongest imprint of Newman and Ignatius —the masters of the real assents that make up the experience of true religion. To understand Hopkins' unique notions of the Romantic spirit, more explanation must be made of his fusion of the views of John Duns Scotus and St. Ignatius as he reconstructed his Christian Romantic version of religious experience.

V

Hopkins' second direct, formal encounter with the Catholic religious tradition occurred when he joined the Society of Jesus. In this religious environment his Romantic state of mind came into fruitful contact with the spiritual methods of St. Ignatius. In Ignatius' *Spiritual Exercises* Hopkins had placed before him the spiritual goal of exercising his religious consciousness to reach his strongest awareness of a God-centered universe. Upon this heightened consciousness he was urged to build deep and lasting attachments within himself to God present in Creation in the person of Jesus Christ. The Society, of course, actively taught St. Ignatius' method of spiritual self-development to achieve these religious goals.

A number of years ago I argued that Hopkins' encounter with the Ignatian meditative method transformed him spiritually into the priest-poet./36/ Now I wish to further that argument by asserting that, in coming upon Ignatius' spiritual methods, Hopkins, to his deep intellectual delight, discovered that Ignatius' process of spiritualizing the personality fit amazingly well with his own account of the energies of the Romantic creative consciousness. Just as the Romantic begins with the I-witness authentication of direct, immediate experience, so Ignatius' meditative method starts with developing the exercitant's capacities to use his *real* experiences as a basis for building transcendent spiritual awareness touching on Christian faith. Since the

25

whole import of Christianity depends upon an imaginative act of historical relocation, the methodology calls upon the exercitant's imagination to "see" Christ present in the world then and now. This use of meditative recollection, I submit, parallels Hopkins' own account of the two energies of the human mind: "The mind has two kinds of energy, a transactional kind, when one thought or sensation follows another, which is to reason . . . ; (ii) an abiding kind for which I remember no name, in which the mind is absorbed (as far as can be), taken up by, dwells upon, enjoys, a single thought: we may call it contemplation, but it includes pleasures, supposing they, however turbid, do not require a transition to another term *of another kind,* for contemplation in its absoluteness is impossible unless in a trance and it is enough for the mind to repeat the same energy on the same matter."/37/ Note Hopkins' emphasis upon this second contemplative energy as a dwelling upon the experience of experiencing, and such delving forestalls any transition into some abstractive mental process or practical act of judgment. So the energy in the Ignatian meditation should not end up in a transfer to some abstract Catholic doctrine; properly exercised, the Ignatian religious mind "dwells," "enjoys," is "absorbed" by its recollective experience of each meditative matter. Ignatius called this state of religious intimacy a colloquy. As a novice, Hopkins could easily have put Ignatius into his own pre-Jesuit terms. In each week of spiritual exercises, the exercitant should "instress" the "scapes" of God as Father, Jesus as His Son, and the Holy Spirit as an expression of their loving, salvific powers actively present in the "inscapes" of the natural world. The meditating mind should attempt to achieve a spiritual "trance" or play of images which involves seeing, associating, fusing, feeling, desiring, giving—the exact amalgam taking a different form in each religious experience. Out of this complex spiritual stage will emerge insights, utterances, and attachments of a deeply felt kind. I suggest that Hopkins found the Ignatian exercise consonant with his account of the Romantic spirit, namely, the full involvement of the whole personality actively penetrating direct experience in a quest for what W. B. Yeats called "Heaven blazing into the head."

But does Ignatius allow for that signal aspect of the Romantic religious imagination, transport to some higher intimations of a transcendent order which mysteriously flood the consciousness with translucent heavenly lights? Transport is clearly a part of the Ignatian meditation. Each exercise in the *Spiritual Exercises* closes with a kind of direct exchange with whatever distinct presence of God appears in the consciousness. Ignatius, in calling this a "colloquy," emphasized that the making of a colloquy involves speaking person to person with the greatest intimacy about one's fears, guilts, desires, and affections. The whole exercise supposes that the exercitant will transport his consciousness to some more personal, real intimation of the Divine Presence through his memory, imagination, and emotions dwelling upon the religious scene called up before the senses. This strong realization of the personal presence of God in the exercitant's experience, a kind of transcendental mystery in which a veil is rent thereby offering extraordinary spiritual sights and insights, is very much like those visionary experiences recorded in the poetry of such Romantics as Blake, Wordsworth, Coleridge, Shelley, and Keats.

Transport and transcendence of this kind can be explained in Hopkins' earlier formulations as a new fusion of intellection and Romanticism, his "new Realism." Hopkins noted that since thought and being are the same, the direct encounter of individual existents by the knowing personality offers the opportunity for the mind to move from the part to the whole, from the individual to the class, from the object to the subject, from the thing to the idea: ". . . knowledge is from the birth upwards . . . ," that is, a gradual ascent to higher and higher awarenesses of the full order of being. However, such transport in the consciousness can be reduced to an abstractive process, for there is the constant danger that the contemplative energy of the mind will break the circuit and get trapped in some repetitive rumination, cut off from its connections with the actualizations of direct experiences. The result is a kind of schism in which experience, ascending awareness, and total understanding lose their vital connections. Hopkins' idea of knowledge demanded a continuity of consciousness in which the entire "knowing" experience matches the continuity of Being. This is what he meant by "new Realism," not a separation of the Rational and the Romantic, not experience versus idea, but rather a unity of consciousness mirroring the Unity of Being. Coleridge, as we have seen, stressed this holistic concept.

Ignatius' method of meditating the Christian religious mysteries has the same basic pattern of developing consciousness which Hopkins conceived as the basic mode of mental contemplative energy. The goal of Ignatian spirituality, to be achieved through the meditative structure of *Spiritual Exercises*, is to "experience" Christ's presence in and through the direct contents of human sensibility. Like Hopkins, Ignatius is unique in his approach to Christian spiritualization in that he grounds his religious regimen in personal sense experience out of which could be generated "from birth upwards" some transport whereby the meditating consciousness reaches some experience "beyond experience," yet within experience. Like the Romantics, Ignatius emphasized the natural order of the religious understanding with great clarity, namely, that recognition comes first, not belief, love first, not faith, assent first, not service. Faith, belief, and service are the rationalizations of recognition, love, and assent. Hopkins found in Ignatius his own confirmation that Being and Thought are one, that through proper contemplation their unity and wholeness can be realized. As he put it:

> The further in anything, as a work of art, the organization is carried out, the deeper the form penetrates, the prepossession flushes the matter, the more effort will be required in apprehension, the more power of comparison, the more capacity for receiving that synthesis of (either successive or spatially distinct) impressions which gives us the unity with the prepossession conveyed by it.
> The saner moreover is the act of contemplation as contemplating that which really is expressed in the object./38/

28

The use of the mind's energy, which Hopkins calls contemplation, then, is a means by which the mind seeks relationships between parts (experience) and wholes (ideas) in order to know a "sense of unity" in the comparison. This thought is Hopkins' version of the Coleridgean Romantic imagination separating and relating, distinguishing and fusing the experience encountered by the consciousness. Since all human experience is successive, the quest, as Hopkins put it, using music as his analogy, is a "synthesis of succession [to] unlock the contemplative enjoyment of the unity as a whole." In Ignatius he found the same thrust of meditative method wherein the exercitant is exhorted to synthesize his religious experience into a recognition of a divine plan for personal salvation.

The contemplative energies of the mind can be misdirected so that the synthesis either is never achieved or breaks down. Hopkins described it thus: "But some minds prefer that the prepossession they are to receive should be conveyed by the least organic, expressive, the most suggestive, way. By this means the prepossession and the definition, uttering, are distinguished and unwound, which is the less sane attitude."/39/ In other words, there is a unificity of Being which the more "sane" mind will discern. Ignatius put it as "the order of things on the face of the earth." Both Hopkins and Ignatius emphasize the continuity of Being which is the quest of true contemplative energy. Both affirm the essential principle of religious Romanticism —the values of the reality of this natural world over any other claims.

It is very plausible to suppose in light of these juxtapositions that young Hopkins, the brilliant Oxford graduate, joyfully discovered within the Church of his newly chosen faith a compatibility beyond anything he might have imagined. Also his new life-long spiritual mentor, the main force in his clerical career, employed a meditative method entirely in accord with his own youthful speculations regarding the meld of full consciousness and transcendent religious experience. Moreover, this coincidence, it is arguable, was to become all the more transforming when it came to relating the poet to the priest, for it was out of the vital connections Hopkins felt in his deep experience of natural beauty that his powerful, expressive, religious imagination grew. To find his Romantic personality seconded by one of the great spiritual masters of the Christian religion meant finding a possible reconciliation between the two sides of his nature—the Romantic artist and the aspiring Christian religious. Indeed the union of the Romantic and Ignatian spirits may have saved the poet in Hopkins. We know how dedicated he was to the spiritualization of his consciousness, so much so that he symbolically burned his poetry to show his readiness to give up, if need be, his Romantic self. However, foregoing his creative personality would probably have been personally devastating, whatever his youthful enthusiasm for his newly found vocation. We know this to be true from the tensions he experienced between priest and poet all through his life. But he was not seeking the absolute denial of his imaginative consciousness; he was seeking to employ the imagination to enlighten and ennoble his religious experience. It must have been marvelous to him that his new spiritual guide counseled in every meditation the use of the imagination in order to realize the presence of Christ in one's spiritual life. Hopkins saw the possibility for the poet of natural beauty to become the priest of supernatural beauty.

The "new Realist" epistemology which Hopkins worked out in his undergraduate days was compatible with the very psychological, meditative methodology Ignatius expressed in his *Spiritual Exercises*. The Ignatian method of meditation involves processes of deepening awareness that presume a continuity of Being and Thought, a unity, discernible in personal experience, that affords a real apprehension of the Divine in the actual contents of direct sensation. If this be not true, then the Ignatian meditation fails in its purpose. To put Ignatius' method in Hopkins' words, somehow the consciousness obtains intimations of Christ's presence in the "stress" of Being. He wrote as an undergraduate: "The truth in thought is Being, stress, and each word is a way of acknowledging Being. . . ."/40/ For Ignatius, of course, truth is ultimately Christ: ". . . when we contemplate Christ our Lord, the representation will consist in seeing in the imagination the natural place." The "natural place" is where Wordsworth, Coleridge, and Ignatius come together. Hopkins sought to "inscape" "me-ness" and "Christ-ness" in his life experiences as a Jesuit poet.

VI

John Robinson, in the most compelling book on Hopkins since Elisabeth Schneider's *Dragon in the Gate*, flatly denies my claim that the Ignatian way is central to Hopkins' development as a poet. He argues that it is Hopkins' "philosophy of form" which he formulated in his undergraduate days which opened up his poetic career. What Robinson is referring to is Hopkins' speculations about the role of organization in any experience whereby the more complex the ordering, the deeper the form of the ordering, the more more difficult the apprehension of experience. In making his case, Robinson draws a comparison between Walter Pater's idea of form and Hopkins' notion. Robinson believes that Hopkins' notion of form seconded by Pater led to his formulation of a working philosophy of art, his invention of the ideas of "inscape" and "instress," even Hopkins' eventual adoption of Scotus' theology. Robinson then brings these viewpoints to bear upon a reading of "The Windhover." In general the argument is impressive and no doubt has much truth in it./41/

However, I suggest that in his quick dismissal of Ignatius, Robinson gives up a vital connection in Hopkins' poetic philosophy. First of all, we must remember that the great poetry Hopkins wrote, he wrote as a Jesuit. Moreover, had he not joined the Society of Jesus, we really cannot know what sort of poet he might have become. Having joined, he produced the poetry we have. We simply cannot dismiss the essential milieu in which he lived, worked, and created most of his adult life. By becoming a Jesuit and living the Jesuit life, all presuppositions are in favor of the Ignatian way of spiritual life shaping in some way his poetic sensibility.

Second, while my earlier statements explaining the Ignatian spirit in Hopkins may not have been fully clear,/42/

31

Robinson, in denying my argument, missed my main assertion, which is that Ignatius gave Hopkins an active, effective method through which to "contemplate" common experience as religious experience; this enabled Hopkins to possess in his creative visions of the natural world recognitions, desires, and assents which could reach spiritually higher and deeper, eventually realizing a specifically Christian affirmation of the mystery of transcendence which the Romantic experience of transport sometime achieved. Third, I held, and still hold,/43/ that the creative process which produces a prayer is parallel with the creative process that makes a poem. Poems are different from prayers, to be sure, but the mental energy that produces them may very well be common. The question is one of imaginative purpose. Ignatius wanted his exercitant to produce a religious utterance, not an esthetic one. However, the shaping, relating, and fusing of experience which goes on in the complex state of consciousness which builds a prayer is surely the religious imagination in action. There must be a creative kinship between this use of the religious imagination and that which produces a religious poem. I asserted this twenty years ago as an argument for the probable impact of the Ignatian method upon Hopkins' poetry. I now affirm even more strongly that the central configuration in Hopkins' religio-poetic consciousness was the Ignation notion of meditation, that is, a dialectical process of creating religious experience by employing the imagination to recreate in the senses a religious image system and to interact with the resultant image pattern in order to develop, in the expressive form of the Ignatian colloquy, personal utterances which touch a broad range of religious feelings, thoughts, and attachments. This Ignatian meditative structure has left its imprint upon the esthetic forms of Hopkins' poetry.

John Robinson denies this influence because he sees no real meaning to the Ignation spirit, no significance to the unique role of the imaginative consciousness in the Ignatian meditation in the long history of the meditative tradition of prayer. Robinson easily bolsters his argument, as have others, by focusing upon the meditative matter which is the object of the Ignatian meditation. He finds Ignatius meditating upon the same Christian matter as other Christian spiritualists, early and late. This unsurprising fact is totally irrelevant to the issue of meditative technique and poetic method. My case rests upon an analysis of the creative epistemology undergirding the Ignatian method. That analysis, I argue, establishes a clear connection between the experience of the creative artistic imagination and the experience of the creative religious imagination. To miss the meaning of the Ignatian spirit as an informing, spiritualizing power shaping the creative consciousness to a deeper realization of Christ subsisting in the human and natural orders is to miss the alloy of religion and art in the language of Hopkins' poetry.

It is not surprising that Robinson sees very little of the specific contents of the *Spiritual Exercises* in Hopkins' poetry. In fact there is very little content in the whole of the *Exercises;* what there is amounts to some exemplary details and particulars in directing the exercitant to focus upon Christian sacral history. It is up to the exercitant to see and feel the life of Christ in personal terms and to draw from these experiences religious thoughts and aspirations leading to spiritual understanding, moral purity, and assents of a deep and abiding charity. It is this method of internalizing the spiritual creativity of the religious consciousness through spiritualizing psychology which, in its dwelling on the sensual mind, intensified by the powers of the religious imagination, is the uniqueness of the Ignatian spirit.

I see the imprint of this meditative methodology, for example, upon "The Windhover." The sonnet is a kind of Ignatian meditative scenario in poetic form, the high point of a contemplative state in which the poetic-religious utterances express sights, sounds, feelings, thoughts, aspirations of beholding Christ "caught" by the religious imagination in the dense flux of natural being.

The first of the three central episodes of the Ignatian meditation—the composition of place—is expressed in the poet's dramatic "catching" the sacramental significance "instressing" the flight of the falcon. The poet-beholder composes (instresses) the bird's natural place (its inscape)

33

through his religious imagination wherein he simultaneously comprehends the person (stress) of Christ present in the majestic creaturehood of the bird. Then follows the second Ignatian meditative episode—the examen of conscience—reflected in the poet–beholder seeing in the curved patterns of the sweeping windhover (answered by the sweep of the skate's heel suggesting a base of universal harmony) the Incarnational fire that powers and illuminates their "inscapes" (air, water, and earth) with sacral meaning, each "selving" the universality of Christ–ness in all creation. What about the poet's Christ-ness?

Following this religio-moral analysis is the third Ignatian episode, that of the colloquy or speaking with God. The Ignatian poet speaks in the fullness of his sanctifying vision of Christ immanent in the very Ur-forms of everything, seeing his Presence, for example, in the furrowing cuts of a plow or the arcing of flashing sparks from a dying fire, echoing the same divine dance as the mirroring movements of the bird and skate. This sublime meeting and greeting enraptures the poet. The recognition pours in on him that all these transient moments of beauty actually embody the Incarnation transforming creation into Christian eternity. The wonder of this vision surcharges the closing colloquy of the sonnet with an assenting love that is deeply felt, indeed, that the "buckling" of all Nature to Christ is the "buckle" of his being. In his rapture the poet-visionary, stirred by this mystery and mastery to a transcending spiritual ecstasy, says, "To Christ our Lord," yes, a thousand times, yes!

Thus we see that the Ignatian meditative mode has become a literary mode; the meditator-poet "looks" at nature "looking back at him; images become words. Religious language is transformed into poetic language. Prayer becomes poetry. In his encounter with Ignatius, Hopkins discovered a vital and profound affirmation of his own Christian Romanticism, a validation which was of immense importance to his two vocations—priest and poet.

VII

Hopkins, however, did have problems on the dogmatic (rationalist) side of his Christianity and the doctrinal tradition of his Jesuit preceptors. These conflicts form the background for his turn to John Duns Scotus, about which more must be said. As a Romantic, Hopkins was committed to the notion that the encounter of natural beauty in direct experience can lead, if informed by a proper spiritualizing state of consciousness—the imaginative intelligence—to a transported experience of supernatural beauty. This powerful intimation is what Hopkins' poetic personality experienced, and it was this kind of experience which he tried to express in most of his poetry. But Hopkins' Romanticism had a special Christian character. For him the true authentication of the Romantic mind lay in penetrating the Incarnation, the union of the "finite" and the "infinite I AM." His spirituality and his poetic experience convinced him that the religious imagination could penetrate to the union of being with Christ. This union reveals, his insight affirmed, that the mundane and the mystical are one.

How can this mystery with the religious consciousness be understood? Hopkins was not satisfied to let the answer to this question remain only intuitive, first, because his strong rational-mindedness, which was forming his "new Realism," sought a psychology for Romanticism to achieve an integrated understanding of reality; and second, because, after becoming a Jesuit, he was being taught a "rationalist" Christian view (Francisco Suarez) which denied that "being in Christ" meant the same "Christ-being in human nature." Suarez affirmed instead, along with most Catholic Scholastics, a more radical discontinuity between Divine and human existence. Such a view blocked religious transport through the creative imagination except by miraculism (see note 44.) The key, as we have seen, to Hopkins' philosophy of Christian Romanticism is the continuity of Being (stress) in all Nature and Divinity, for each is opposed to nothingness in the same way. If the same principle of being exists in God as in Nature, the "scapes" of the material world do reveal their Divine occupation. Even before he became a Jesuit, Hopkins perceived the long tradition of rationalists arguing for the descending version of realism: "Realism will undoubtedly once more maintain that the Idea is only given —whatever may be the actual form education takes—from the whole downwards to the parts."/44/ Romanticism called for an epistemology dependent upon an ascending "form of education from the part to the whole," what Hopkins called a "new Realism." This view allowed for the "stress" in "scapes" to be traced from mortal to immortal being. This was the key notion as well to Ignation meditation—finding Christ "selving" in the flux of human nature by pondering the translucent Christ-self in natural and human history.

Hopkins needed some philosopher in the great tradition of Catholic thought who rescued the intensity of the Romantic personality, who corroborated the personalist character of the Ignation meditation, and who allowed for a role for the sanctifying imagination to find and express real and vital connections between all three components, "a repetition in the finite mind of the eternal act of creation in the infinite I AM," to quote Coleridge. Scotus more than filled the need (see note 45). Scotus posited a concept of univocal being throughout all existence; he held that created nature is a personification of Christ who sums up all existential degrees indigenous to common, visible nature. If this understanding is true, then it is possible for ordinary human consciousness to apprehend the individual, the type, and the archetype in experiencing the natural world. Scotus called this knowledge a kind of "vision of existence" in which the consciousness is transported into a visionary, imaginative state to glimpse the Unity of all Being—an ascent from partness to wholeness revealing the relationships between common and particular nature in the great scale of Being, the totality expressing the Incarnation "as the eternal act of creation." A glimpse of divinity could occur because all natural things are not derivations of the Creator; rather everything is a direct participant in God's existence. Creator and creation are bonded in the same being. Every created thing, therefore, while possessing its own "inscape" or individuality, at the same time is a finite image of the infinite image of its maker. It follows, then, that every "inscape," be it a word, a thing, or a person, each and all express Christ's presence.

36

It is in Hopkins' commentary on the *Spiritual Exercises* that he merged Ignatius and Scotus most evidently. A significant instance of how Hopkins observed the same sense of reality in his two great sages can be seen in his remarks about the great meditation which closed the *Exercises*, the "Contemplation to Attain the Love of God." In this exercise Ignatius directs the exercitant to realize God's love in all his actions. To accomplish this, Ignatius reminds the exercitant of the sharing nature of love, of how much God has given him, and how much he ought to give back. These reflections lead to the high point of the meditation, the offering of oneself to the Lord, expressed in the famous prayer, "Take, Lord, and receive all my liberty, my memory, my understanding, and my entire will, all that I have and possess."

In his commentary, Hopkins gives a very Scotian analysis. He stresses the point that love is essentially a "giving and a communicating to the beloved." How can this be? Hopkins explains: "God dwells in creatures: in the elements giving them being; in the plants giving them growth; in the animals giving them sensation; in men giving them understanding; and so in me giving me being, life, sensation, and causing me to understand; making likewise of me a temple, since I am created to the likeness and image of his Divine Majesty" (*Sermons*, 193). Hopkins' emphasis upon the notion that the being in all things, specially in him, is the same being in God, sets up a Scotian vision of existence in which God's being is "selving," "speaking," "playing" in and through every individual thing.

Later Hopkins comments on Ignatius' point about God keeping His promises: "In particular He has suffered in the flesh as man, the Word but really made flesh. His presence is a reality though invisible; Nature has a real stability, His providence is active, air, food, and clothing [and so on] will not run out during our lifetime; these copies of His perfection are the merest shadows, the reality beggars the expectation. Hence it turns out that though God gives us His Word and Image, the Word and Image has with it the divine substance" (*Sermons*, 194). For Hopkins, then, reaching the Word and Image meant exercising the sanctifying imagination. In this way the poet takes on a priestly role, for poetry selves self and Christ. No wonder the words of awe in the opening stanza of "The Wreck of the Deutschland": "And dost thou touch me afresh? / Over again I feel thy finger and find thee."

A Scotian sense of reality abounds in Hopkins' comments about Ignatius. As notable are the number of instances when religious comment becomes poetic illustration. A fine example of this is Hopkins' final comment on "the contemplation of the Holy Spirit sent to us through creatures." This meditation focuses on the Holy Spirit as the love between the Father and the Son and therefore between God and mankind. This love is communicated, he noted, through "the works of God's fingers." Thus again Hopkins emphasizes the Scotian modality of the Word and the Image in his closing comments on Ignatius' meditation on attaining love. Indeed his final statement of Scotian reality is transformed by his sanctifying imagination: "All things therefore are charged with God and if we know how to touch them give off sparks and take fire, yield drops and flow, ring and tell of him" (*Sermons*, 195). These lines illustrate the immediacy of God's presence according to St. Ignatius, the immanence of Christ according to Scotus, and the rich transformation of religious colloquia into poetry by Hopkins, the priest-poet. The next step might be a poem like "God's Grandeur." Hopkins' commentary on Ignatius' "Contemplation to Attain the Love of God" exhibits his sanctifying imagination in full operation.

In sum, it is Scotus' emphasis on a Christ-centered Nature and the possibility of "catching" His presence in and throughout common experience that Hopkins affirmed as the Christian philosophical linchpin of his "new Realism." Here was a major Catholic theologian providing a far better account of the spiritual transport aimed at in the meditations of Ignatius, as Hopkins understood them, than his current Jesuit preceptors. According to Scotus, the exercitant could labor at "seeing" Christ in the transporting "spots of time," as Wordsworth called them, because it was possible for an intuitive vision to be opened up which afforded a true glimpse of Christ in created nature. Thus the Jesuit Romantic poet could see God's face in any dappled thing: ". . . just then when I took in any inscape of the sky or sea I thought of Scotus."/45/ Romanticism, reason, meditation, Christianity, priesthood, and poetry might all fit together into some creative synthesis. Hopkins' Jesuit life to a major extent was centered on the realization of this grand, unifying understanding. As he wrote in a comment on St. Ignatius using Scotus: "That is Christ *being me* and me being Christ."

The essential character of Hopkins' synthesis for a "new Realism" grew primarily out of his thinking about art generally and his own writing of poetry. Art and poetry were the frame of his philosophic speculations from the beginning. In one set of notes, for example, Hopkins began with locating the nature of language in his system of mental energies: "For the word is the expression, *uttering* of the idea in the mind." He went on to distinguish the poetic word from the intellectual word: ". . . the image (of sight or sound or *scapes* of the other senses), which is in fact physical and a refined energy [that is when deliberately formed or when a thought is recalled, for when produced by sensation from without or when as in dreams, etc., it presents itself unbidden, it comes from the involuntary working of nature] accenting the nerves, a word unto itself, an inchoate word. . . ."/46/ The other word produced by the mind is the conception word of the abstractive, intellective process. Hopkins thought that each word is produced by two kinds of mental energies, "a transitional kind" and "an abiding kind."/47/ One power is creative energy which Romantics describe as symbolic and the other defining energy which rationalists cite as concepts. However, these two energies, according to Hopkins, following Coleridge, are not mutually exclusive. Art, for example, employs both: ". . . even in successive arts as music, for full enjoyment, the synthesis of the succession should give, unlock, the contemplative enjoyment of the unity of the whole. . . . Works of art of course utter the idea and in representing real things convey the prepossession with more or less success."/48/ The *word*, then, according to Hopkins, is part of the unity of Being and Thought, as image and conception. Art and poetry are produced by a complex, creative use of these mental energies.

This analysis of Hopkins' thinking outlines a rudimentary formulation of his philosophy of art in the guise of a "new Realism"—"chromatic beauty." I think it defensible to suggest that the operative base of Hopkins' creativity is this philosophy of art I have outlined, from which he proposed to try to create a different and new kind of Christian Romantic poetry. In such a poetry the poet utters the full spectrum of the creative consciousness—the "catching of the inscape" of some natural, visible object, the "instressing" of its "scape" to the level of a kind of complex multiple awareness in which the individual thing is seen in a scale of existents, and, on inspired occasions, through a kind of refinement of imaginative energy, the occurrence of some rare, transcendent, visionary sight or insight into a higher order of Being—the Incarnation. In writing such poetry, Hopkins wished to do more than record and confess his own experience, as do many Romantic artists; he sought to penetrate existence deeply, to the level of Being itself. In these awesome moments of transported consciousness, the Incarnation seemed to come to full realization in him as a song of mortal and immortal beauty.

I realize that in asserting that Hopkins had developed what amounts to a settled theory of art rests on my own synthesis. He wrote no fully developed philosophic statement of his own on art, so far as we know. His essay on Platonic beauty is as close as he came. What we have are some brilliantly speculative remarks in some undergraduate essays, some complex jargon, and some very provocative ideas scattered here and there which are fraught with rich implications for fuller development. Unfortunately, for the most part, Hopkins left us to pursue the philosophic implications of his statements on art on our own. His whole life and work has the weakness of incompleteness so far as any finished, formal statement of his definitive understanding of most of these issues so important to him. His "lonely begans" are among the major problems any biographer must face. Nevertheless, what he did express amounts, I am arguing, to a firm sketch of a basic philosophic position which I have called Christian Romanticism, a kind of synthesis of the imaginative and intellectual energies of the consciousness focusing upon the uses of the religious imagination generally and the production of religious poetry specifically.

What Hopkins aimed for in his poetry was to express with the greatest individuality the phenomenology of his "new Realism." Dramatizing the forces of this dialectical synthesis meant fusing the two energies of the contemplating mind—reasoning and imagining—through the unifying powers of "word scapes." The unifying key to his capturing effectively the two basic contemplative powers of the mind was the creation of a new, poetic word order which would somehow express what happens to creative consciousness when experiencing the raptures of transport to an original, new witnessing of Divinity (Incarnation) present in the world. His powerful poetic nature led him to seek some fresh, expressive form which would take directly the imprint of his Christian Romantic account of the upper creative consciousness—Christ-play "inscaped" in a new poetic language.

We know that he tried a mix of traditional English and Classical prosody in his second version of his poem of St. Dorothea, but we know little more. Suddenly, it seems, though surely it must have been otherwise, a new poetic form bursts forth in "The Wreck of the Deutschland," for which we have no poetic precedents in his early writings. In this first major poem written in his new esthetic, Hopkins set out to give full-blown expression to his "new Realism." In this poem, "stress" and "scape" are fused in an original statement of Christian-Romantic consciousness. These two fundamental dynamics of Being take on a more perfect union reflecting the conjunction of the mind's energies penetrating Being while mirroring Being. Hopkins' mature poetry is a kind of horizontal and vertical icon of creative consciousness. In realizing such poetry, Hopkins was reaching for "deeper" artistic form. "The further in anything, as a work of art, the organization is carried out, the deeper the form penetrates, the prepossession flushes the matter, the more effort will be required in apprehension. . . ."/49/ "Deeper" form is what he sought in his poetry, for only by achieving such a richness of poetic form could he reflect the complex organization of the kind of religious consciousness he wished to write about. "Deep" form esthetically meant word density, image clotting, irregular rhythms, daring elisions, and heavily packed meaning. If

41

such charged "word scapes" could be achieved, then his poems would possess what he called "synthesis of impres-sion" and "unity with the prepossessions conveyed by it." Poetry possessing this unique character was what Hopkins aimed to produce.

John Robinson argues that this "deeper" form is the key to Hopkins' growth as a poet./50/ However, we disagree as to the major shaping forces behind this poetic principle. He discusses Hopkins' encounter with Walter Pater's idea of form to show that both rested their basic philosophic vision in some concept of form though Hopkins would not limit his ideas to sensible form only. While I do not deny some influ-ence from Pater, especially his affirmation of expressive form as the major force of the creating consciousness, as I have asserted heretofore, Hopkins' idea of expressive form was modified in a major way by his contact with Ignatius and Scotus. Pater affirmed for Hopkins the idea of artistic form as a deep structure, but Ignatius and Scotus were the influences which provided the solution to esthetic atomism.

The differences between Hopkins and Pater are impor-tant. Pater did not assert any necessary connection between Being and Thought, as did Hopkins, with the result that Pater's idea of the mind's consciousness is a kind of perpetual motion machine struggling to discover some mode whereby the kaleidoscope of sensation connects with reality. This disunion gives rise to only momentary connec-tive relationships; the consciousness slips into isolated quests which surround the personality in a thick crust of sensations, impenetrable and imprisoning. To Pater, form is essentially a subjective imprint upon sensation, a kind of attempt to congeal sensation into some purely esthetic pattern having no secure connections with the deep struc-ture of reality. This notion of esthetic form is sometimes called pure Romanticism because of its subjective char-acter, but in Hopkins' terms it is a "failed" Romanticism ("diatonic beauty") because such roving sensibility is subject to all the sloppy, sentimental self-authentications which are the mental squalor of many Romantics at one time or another. The same fate can be the result of a fuller Roman-tic mentality when consciousness reaches no transport and thus no transcendental understanding. Pater grasped the inadequacy of his notion of form and sought to make it "deeper" through some sort of sensible transport but with no conviction about any valid connections between consciousness and being. This yearning for a center for "deep" form occurs in much of his writing, but nowhere more evidently than in his *Marius the Epicurean*, wherein he tries to express a kind of transporting aspiration for a version of natural Christianity./51/ However, the contemplating consciousness never achieves a valid, convincing, personal affirmation of the religious imagination in *Marius*, nor for that matter does Pater ever achieve an expression of the genuine religious imagination in any of his writings. Pater remained a Platonic esthete locked into his own evanescent mental mannerisms, whereas Hopkins is a new Parmenides celebrating the high energy consciousness of a new unity of "I am" with "it is or there is." Unlike Pater, Hopkins never confused Being with the mind and therefore never mixed up art and life, esthetics and religion. On this John Robinson and I totally agree: "Hopkins' comments on 'form' are not confined to art; they may be true of 'anything.' "/52/

VIII

We are now ready to ask about the special character of the "deeper" form which Hopkins gave to his mature poetry. The approach I have been suggesting calls for an answer which best might be termed "Christ-scaping," that is, a poetic attempt to realize the ideal of the Christian religious imagination—the rendering in authenticating esthetic form the felt perceptions of God (Christ) in real experience. The means necessary to achieve this artistic ideal must involve the actualization of the fullest powers of contemplative transport that can be organized by the creative imagination; the poetry produced is a poetry of sublimity. To be valid such poetic expression must have birth in the actuality of direct and immediate experience from and through which the transcendent consciousness achieves its transport. Such a creative affirmation is the highest production of the Romantic imagination. It is precisely in realizing this new consciousness that Romanticism has caused a profound shift in the significance of religious experience in general and Christianity in particular.

Romanticism in its most essential meaning is a form of religious experience. The credentials of the highest aspirations of the Romantic consciousness are direct encounter with real experience and the penetration of such experience to the depth of some deeper experience beyond natural experience. At its most sublime moments, the Romantic imagination captures sights and insights of some Presence of a Center from which all existence seems to flow and which all being strains to realize. When this happens, the Romantic consciousness becomes religious and its creative expressive forms reverential, meditative, and humble. Some subjective expression of religion based upon real experience has challenged, some would say invalidated, the traditional rationalist approach to the "knowing" of God as a featureless concept described in abstract negatives. This "spilling" of religion into Romanticism is far more general than is usually acknowledged. I have in other writings tried to trace this shift to a Romantic religious consciousness in Pater, Kingsley, and Newman, all of whom have attempted to depict the experience of some awareness of the Incarnation authenticated in real experience in their religious novels./53/ In each of these works, the authors attempted to rely upon the imagination in meditative transport to glean some perception of a Deity featured as real and concrete in actual experience. I suggested that these novels of religious discovery, each in its own way, are efforts to achieve an esthetic expression of the religious ideal I have described as "Christ-scaping." I use this term, it should be noted, in its broadest sense and do not limit it to Catholicism alone. Such esthetic statements of "Incarnationalism" as a phenomenon of real and direct experience, of course, resist any strictly rational analysis or declaration, reject any "God of negative transcendence," and deny the devaluation of religious experience as the foundation of true faith.

Romantic "Incarnationalism"/54/ I would describe as dependent upon two perceptive constants to be authentic: all existence must possess a continuity of real being throughout all its orders and levels, including thought and

44

word, and the manifestations of this continuous, real being must be susceptible to imaginative apprehension to the depth of encounter with some omnipotent presence presiding at the center of existence. As we have already seen, Hopkins, influenced by the modalities of Ignatius and Scotus, affirmed "stress" and "scape" as his way of validating these two real principles in his own experience.

Let us now bring all of this analysis to bear upon Hopkins' mature poetry. Essentially what I will be attempting throughout the rest of this essay is to examine key poems in Hopkins' canon to see whether, as I have argued, each poem in varying degrees is an attempt of Hopkins' religious imagination to realize in esthetic form the meta-experiences of the transported Romantic consciousness. We will begin by looking into the "deeper form" of "The Wreck of the Deutschland."

In this great ode, all the more astounding because it seems to have sprung from Hopkins suddenly and spontaneously, there is a two-part structure to the form. The poem is basically about the poet's fabulous journey to contact God. The extended metaphor the poet used to elucidate his spiritual quest is heroism. Describing the ode in Hopkins' own poetic philosophy, we might say he imaginatively fused the "scapes" of his own Ignatian meditative experience in all of its exalted spiritual transcendence with the "scapes" he gleaned from the *Deutschland* tragedy, especially the story of the tall nun. The entire poem turns on a kind of metaphorical "hypostasis" in the form of the poem. Just as he had "I-witnessed" Christ in his own direct and immediate religious experience (Part the First), so it was possible that the tall nun experienced during her travail the same religious transport to some higher consciousness in which she achieved a direct impression of some rescuing Deific Presence. Hopkins imaginatively fused his real spiritual transport with a similar experience he imagined for the "tall nun" in order to achieve the basic expressive form of his ode.

His prime aim was to "inscape" his own religious experience and ultimately all such experience. His creative

45

effort generated images through the intensity of his contemplative artistic energy which range the whole terrain of the mental landscape of religious transport in an attempt to express the sights and insights that led him to a transcendent sense of some truly felt intimation of the Lord.

Central to such an artistic endeavor of trying to put in esthetic, expressive form the most ethereal of human experiences is finding the artistic word formula which can express the dynamics of such intense meditative energy, capture the sweep of powerful emotions, and keep in the foreground the human sense of reality that is the arena of real experience. This is a very high ideal for religious poetry; thus Hopkins' Christian-Romantic artistic consciousness required a fresh, new, commanding poetic. I believe this is why Hopkins tried to employ poetic language which was grounded in oral speech, but which at the same time, through the management of pauses and stresses (pauses especially because he was dealing with mystic exaltations on the breathless mountaintops of the mind) elevates the poetic statements into an original kind of surcharged language which can tell of, indeed does possess, the "scape" and "stresses" of truly elevated religious experience. The ultimate result is a unique poetic line, in which there is such a powerful sense of verbal pitch that the poem calls for readers who nearly intone the poem, much as a singer intones the pitch of musical scores.

"The Wreck" is a startling first instance of Hopkins' "new Realist" Romantic consciousness in artistic action. This is to say that the "deeper form" of the poem is truly unique, distinctly original, not only, I submit, because of its use of "sprung rhythm" and Hopkins' penchant for purer Anglo-Saxon words, but also because the poetic form is a verbal structuring of an extraordinary level of religious consciousness that I have called "Christ-scaping," the esthetic equivalent of Incarnationalism. In fact Hopkins himself knew the unusualness of his poetic matter and said as much in Stanza 6 wherein he openly addresses the "stress" of God upon nature and human nature in all of its terror and awe. Once this creative-expressive notion of "Christ-scaping" is grasped, as the Jesuits at *The Month* and Robert

46

Bridges did not, the poem opens up to wondrous richness. Far from being a "dragon" at the gate of Hopkins' work, it is more like Blake's burning tiger evoking us to dare frame the symmetry of human consciousness in a visionary state of religious sublimity.

I am not saying that the entire poem is always at the heights of religious, imaginative sublimity, of course, but its inspirational powers stay at a high level for a long narrative poem. "The Wreck" opens with a surprisingly surcharged account of the drama of the transported religious consciousness. The poet begins with the religious experience of "finding" God and goes on to depict the marvel of such a discovery. His primary focus is upon the contents of such a religious consciousness experiencing this awesome event—sights, sounds, things, desires, choices, fears, joys—realizing in the fullest sense Ignatius' spiritual direction "to see the place." In expressing the marvel of "Christ-scaping" in heightened religious experience, the poet is dramatizing how wonderful, how terrible, how consequential, how transforming, how ultimate is such an event in the spiritualized consciousness. In doing so he almost loses us in such difficult lines as "To flash from the flame to the flame. . . ." In fact what has happened to him is finally inexpressible, and Part the First, therefore, is more a celebration of the I-witness than a description of the witnessed. Part the Second is really an attempt to try to express what has happened in Part the First in more general, common human terms—how God enters time, experience, consciousness. These "explanations," of course, have artistic purpose as well, for they make of the shipwreck an "objective correlative" where the poet can poetically ruminate on what has happened to him.

The poet's attempt to project his experience of "Christ-scaping" is the main effort of the poem. Had he opted for a one-part form, the poem would have been a powerful poetic statement of the religious imagination at a sublime level of excitement. By developing a two-part form, Hopkins risked much. One liability was a lowering of spiritual intensity. He tried to make up for this reduction of religious imagination by his handling of the drama of the shipwreck. Though brilliantly done, the passages do not arise from the same inspiring religious energies which fueled the first part of the poem. On the way to locate and express the "Christ-scape" consciousness in Part the Second, the prime narrative goal in this segment, there are stanzas which contribute only obliquely to this end. These "asides" tend to siphon off the tension building in the poem that was needed to dramatize a second instance of the religious mind at a very high level of transcendent religious awareness.

The poet begins his approach to that awesome moment of "finding" God in the *Deutschland* event (Part the Second) in Stanza 17 when he introduces the figure of a rising "lioness," and in Stanza 18 he tries to underscore the oncoming momentous event by describing his own excitement about what was happening. In Stanza 19, the poet again picks up the shipwreck drama which is the "objective correlative" to the altar and the night in Part the First. Then, surprisingly, he pulls back and introduces three stanzas which slacken the religious tension, hold off the moment of spiritual recognition, stanzas which embroider the narrative situation usefully but which decidedly are typological "asides" to his theme of "Christ-scaping." These are Stanza 20, "She was first of a five," Stanza 21, "Loathed for a love men knew in them," Stanza 22, "Five, the finding and the sake," and Stanza 23, "Joy fall to thee, Father Francis." Only after these stanzas does he take up his fabulous conjecture again. These stanzas seem poetic "fillers," that is, passages that arise not from direct and immediate experience, but rather from a kind of intellectualization of the situation, perhaps inevitable in a long poem organized around a complex and rare state of consciousness, but nevertheless meditative embellishments apart from the dramatic center of the ode. Had I played Pound to Hopkins, I would have removed Stanzas 20, 22, and 23 as not sufficiently contributive to his religious drama. While they are not blotches by any means, these ornamental passages are "slacks" in that dramatic intensity which was established so breathlessly in the first part of the poem and which the second part needs in order to make the ode's two-part structure balance in poetic energy.

It can be conjectured that it was precisely this kind of "objective correlative" problem which caused Hopkins to turn mainly to the sonnet as his prime poetic form. He in fact may have discovered in this first long ode the limits of esthetic form in expressing the sort of contemplative energies he was attempting. Perhaps the "Christ-scapes" of the kind of religious experience he was trying to put into poetic form needed a more concentrated structure where the inner formal tensions of the verbal form can more readily mirror the spontaneous pressures of direct experience at a very high level of spiritual concentration. Whatever the reason, most assuredly the sonnet became the essential poetic "scape" of Hopkins' imaginative religious consciousness.

All readers agree that Stanza 28 is the high point of the second part of "The Wreck." How different from the matching passages in Part the First! After having dramatically announced in the opening stanza of the ode that he felt God's "touch," Hopkins in the following two stanzas attempts to depict those moments in his religious consciousness during which he "saw" his Masters' face and "felt" transported to some dazzling encounter with God Himself. These passages attempt to recapture those elevated points in but beyond time-consciousness, to celebrate them, to examine them, to perpetuate them. The time complex (both natural and psychological) is made evident in the dominating tenses in each stanza. Stanza 1 is the extended present, Stanzas 2 and 3 time past (but timeless in a sacral sense), Stanzas 4 and 5 the immediate present, and Stanza 6, 7, and 8 the historical present, Stanzas 9 and 10, the vocative present. The key to the time pattern is the Incarnation in motion. So besides startling his reader with the extraordinary revelations about the experiences of his own religious consciousness, Hopkins also places his momentous religious encounters in both a personal and universal historical frame. The importance of doing this was vital if the ode were to lay out the Christian plan of salvation. First, it was important to elucidate the sacral time cycle of Christ, and second, it was critical to show how the sacral abides within the natural time cycle as "Christ-scapes." By locating this crucial connection, Hopkins' imagination authenticated his own heightened religious experience and offered the same authentication to the tall nun on the *Deutschland* (and by metaphoric extension to all those on the wrecked ship who answered her call). The poet "read right" the time "scape" (the juxtaposition of natural, psychological, and sacral time) of the two wrecks. At some point they become centered on each other as moments of special religious intimation. Those moments were those in which a properly disposed religious consciousness leapt up through the immediate data of the senses to another level of consciousness, and from this elevation saw in the natural predicament a new relationship to some higher order of existence, the shape of which can only be called an illuminative Presence producing the most powerful effect upon the entire episode. So compelling to the beholder is the experience that he becomes part of a visionary company. Such an event is at the very heart of the Romantic consciousness, and the dramatized recollection of such an event is the very essence of the Romantic imagination in recreative action as we have seen. What Hopkins is saying is that immortal beauty is contactable in and through the visionary flight of the human consciousness "instressing" Divinity out of mortal beauty.

In Part the Second, Hopkins attempted to affirm imaginatively for the tall nun what he had affirmed actually in Part the First—that he had met God Himself. However, in depicting the nun's experience, he had to express the matter "at arm's length," so to speak. This accounts, I believe, for the differences between his witnessing his own experience and telling the nun's. Especially, I believe, projecting his own "spot of time" into her imagined religious mind caused him to handle her visionary moment differently. Not being able to rely on direct experience, he had to conjecture poetically about the process of her religious consciousness as he does in Stanzas 25, 26, and 27. What did she mean when she called, "O Christ, Christ come quickly?" The poet wanted inspiration, "arch and original Breath." But it didn't come; he could not enter into the rising whirlpool of her religious consciousness by means of the "leads" he attempted to trace—her deep love for God, Scripture, a kind of overwhelming sudden baptism of desire, or tears or terrors. To what real or imagined Presence she spoke, and whether there was a reply, remains a mystery. But the poet, knowing what he himself saw and felt, proposes her as a metaphor for his own hallowed moment of recognition. She was an "objective correlative" for his own awesome religious epiphany, a most attactively rich religious poetic figure. Unlike his "safe" ascent to a still center of religious affirmation, she stood and called out for rescue amid stormy death. What religious heroism! What spiritual derring-do! What a test of love and trust! What an authentication of faith! Whether it was really all of these is not important. What is important is that the poet found the metaphor for his own "yes / O at lightning and lashed rod." She "worded" his great religious assent in a way that went beyond a hidden confirming instance; she provided a new assent, namely, the rebirth of Hopkins' poetic imagination as an expressive vehicle for his religious consciousness. No wonder that the poet played upon "wording," "word," "worded," right after the dramatic metaphoric moment in Stanza 28: "There then! the Master, . . ." Of course, it is appropriate to take up St. John and play the gospel through the text at this point./55/ It makes sense theologically, spiritually, and artistically. But the nun's call as the poet's metaphor for his own assent to a transported religious experience is more; it is the emancipation of the poet. She was the Simon Peter of Hopkins' poetic soul. Without taking away any of the religious glosses in these passages, I submit that in their deepest structure they tell of a new release for the poet's religious imagination, a new quest for his poetry, a new purpose for his creative personality. This new Mary, whatever she had conceived spiritually and whatever she delivered when the moment came, surely conceived the poet's "brain / Word, that heard and kept thee and uttered thee outright." What more is there to say except to hope for the real authenticity for the metaphor, that she truly "has thee for the pain . . ."? The poet had his heart freed to sing his/her hosannahs.

All readers do not agree, however, on the reading of Stanza 28. John Robinson, for example, confirms Elisabeth Schneider's reading of this stanza as a depiction of a miracle by which the tall nun saw Christ./56/ This is a plausible reading if one takes a strictly rationalist approach to such

51

poetry, thereby denying what Northrup Frye calls "the point of epiphany" between nature and the apocalyptic world as having any authenticity. Also such a reading point of view discountenances Hopkins' "Christ-scaping" as a real, epiphanic point in the development of religious consciousness. I have been arguing, of course, that no miracle in the accepted theological sense is expressed anywhere in the poem. The only "miracle" is that of the imagination, in which the poet imagines the nun in the circumstances of a transporting religious experience in which she "sees" her Master present in the very actuality of the shipwreck, and by virtue of this visionary imaginative act, the poet transforms her call into a higher, symbolic, religious truth.

To readers who do not accept the testament of such translucent religious vision, which is the very root of all true Romanticism, such a possibility is so wondrous that it can only be explained by some form of alleged miraculism. As William Blake asserted so powerfully in all his writings and engravings, human consciousness is grounded in the "here" while touching the "beyond." Such transcendental transport is the very essence of the visionary, Romantic religious consciousness. The real drama lies with the God-seeker. the champions in "The Wreck" are the poet and the nun, not God-Christ. While the poet makes theologically clear whose the ultimate power is, he makes dramatically evident how powerful is the religious consciousness of aspirants whose beauty and beauty-making powers can "say yes" or "read the unshapeable shock night."

Vision to the point of epiphany is the highest exponential power of what Coleridge called the "translucent" Romantic imagination. Miracle in the sense that secular readers use it denies the visionary imagination. John Robinson asserts that Hopkins attempted to use the *deus ex machina* of the miracle to rescue the second half of the poem for the sake of "pietist reveries," even to the point of neglecting to express the terror and destruction that the wreck meant for all the others on board./57/ If, as Robinson asserts, Stanza 28 is a "poetic" miracle and all that follows is mere pietism, Hopkins stands guilty as charged. But if one is open to at least esthetic membership in the visionary company which the poet assembles, then the hope that the poet expresses, born of charity and sanctified by common assent, becomes a possibility full of redemptive plenitude. Indeed the poet's expanded heart is full of sympathy for all the shipwrecked, ". . . but pity the rest of them! Heart, go and bleed at a bitterer vein for the / Comfortless unconfessed of them"; he hopes for the inclusion of all "the poor sheep" through the salvific powers of his apocalyptic vision. Readers like Robinson, and R. F. Leavis before him, limit the poem to an esthetic suspension of disbelief making the Incarnational symbolism merely a poetic device whose adequacy is measured in terms of maintaining imaginatively the realism of the catastrophe. I submit such a response is a serious misreading of the poem, that in such reading the poem is reduced to the single world of secular Nature whereas the poem is really about the circumstances that surround the alignment of the apocalyptic world with the world of Nature. Moreover, misreading those central stanzas surrounding Stanza 28 in Part the Second leads to such a literary upset of the metaphorical system in the ode that the last four stanzas become mere poetic exercise. To such readers, the last stanzas are not a great hymning of the mysteries of the Lord discovered; rather they are, as Robinson states, merely a "set piece; beyond this in any direction, emotionally, intellectually, or spiritually, we may not go. . . ."/58/ Robinson is here saying that the poet has failed to endow his poem with more than mere poetic ornaments. Of course, what we really have here is a "great divide" between those readers who share Hopkins' religious consciousness and those who do not. I do fault, however, Robinson's criticisms from the point of view of a nonsharer. Any reader who finds himself falling on the underside of such visionary religious poetry should have written, I submit: ". . . beyond this in any direction, emotionally, intellectually, or spiritually, [I] may not go. . . ." Such a critical stance is one of proper critical humility before a considerable host of readers who experience a different state of poetic consciousness in the poem. The difference is vital between the two critical points of view. Every effort must always be made to keep open avenues of mutual apprehension between those who make up one readership and those who make up the other. In reality we are all the same readers who can at least recognize that the poem climaxes in a song of jubilant praise and celebration whose carol inspires every reader to join in the chorus of Christ's mastering love and the mystery of its saving powers amidst the "wrecks" of soul and body in this world. Even readers who suffer a kind of shipwreck on the words of the last stanza of the poem can perceive the holy wishes expressed in these passages and hope that they might be so. There is, I submit, an unconscious Christian hope in every reader's heart. Finally, as Norman MacKenzie notes in his Hopkins *Reader's Guide* when talking about this last stanza, "The imagery which warms the final and crowded lines of the poem brings out the willing welcome and heart-felt respect He should be accorded." No reader can miss this tone of generous hospitality.

IX

The basic substructure of the new kind of religious poetry which Hopkins was trying to write has now been uncovered. His psycho–drama of the imaginative religious intellect produces a unique state of spiritual consciousness best expressed in some poetic form. The religious experience that is fastened in the expressed form involves seeing the "thisness" in the things that comprise the experience upon which the contemplative energies of the mind, if rightly ordered, generate a kind of transported insight beyond the limits of natural vision. However, this vertical movement in the consciousness still inheres in the throng of sense experience, especially sight, and elicits from the emotions religious feelings of affirmation, celebration and exhortation, all of which become the substance of each poem. The deeper structure of Hopkins' poetry is thus shaped by the creative–expressive forces of such a religious consciousness in an exalted state of transcendental vision. Not all of his poetry was produced out of this highly spiritual mentality, of course, but the poetry most characteristic of his poetic genius is at some "point of epiphany" within the religious consciousness. The pattern of perception, response, and transcendence dramatized so powerfully in Hopkins' poetic language suggests that most of Hopkins' poetry was written at a very elevated state of spiritual inspiration.

Looking at the poems which followed Hopkins' ode on the *Deutschland,* we find instances of a very transported religious consciousness, perhaps because of his having arrived at a new synthesis of poetic form and religious experience, and being flushed with the richness of his own personal religious experience as a newly ordained priest full of holiness and zeal. These poems of religious bliss cannot all be discussed in detail here in order to elucidate their deeper religio-poetic form. However, some general attributes can be usefully noted.

One aspect of this kind of religious poetry is its distinctive imaginative engagement with Nature. More than other Romantic poets, Hopkins concentrated on the uniqueness of individual entities in Nature. He saw a world in each thing in Nature's panoply which led him to attempt to discover a unifying metaphysic which accounts for these very accurate observations. He wanted a metaphysic that stressed unique being, "thisness," in its system of existential principles. Scotus' understanding of "thisness" was as close as Hopkins could come within the Christian philosophic tradition to his visionary, dramatic affirmation of individuality in his notion of the "inscape" of things portending some divine "instress." This plane of particularized Nature, dense with the beauty of natural "inscapes," can be itself a source of a kind of original Romantic poetry that expresses Nature flooding the sensitive-imaginative systems. Such poetry is the staple of the Romantic canon. In such poetry some aspect of Nature's individual expression is animated to the level of human personification at which point the poet enters into the cycle of natural life to find the harmony or disharmony of the human and the natural. Romantic poetry is replete with this type of poem. The poetic consciousness remains fixated in a kind of rapport in the felt pleasures of natural beauty. For Hopkins such a poetic rapture, while intensely absorbing and moving, is a very limited, evanescent state of Romantic consciousness because of the ever-constant change in Nature, the limitations in the human sensory system, and the inefficiency of contemplative mental energies. Hopkins produced some fine poems at this first level of Romantic consciousness—"Penmaen Pool," "Binsey Poplars," "Inversnaid," "Ribblesdale."/59/ These poems are examples of the Romantic imagination at its median level on the way to a full-blown Romantic consciousness. The Romantic imaginative intellect in these poems is content to penetrate only to the level of the world's body.

The Romantic poems in which Nature is apprehended mainly at the level of the sensory spectrum are not always positive in tone. In fact, the poems of this kind that Hopkins wrote, while lovingly descriptive, are more often than not sadly melancholic with much feeling of the mortality of natural beauty. The "stress" expressed in these poems is that of a single-dimensioned Nature whose beauties are mechanically vanishing, or worse, whose glories are being additionally despoiled by human insensitivity and destructiveness. How to prevent the experience of Nature from disintegrating into subject and object, Nature's beauty from dwindling into biological mechanics, and the bond between the beholding human consciousness and the radiant organism of Nature's order from becoming an alienating state of desolating isolation are perhaps the prime challenges of such a Romantic consciousness. Mutability is the fate of human experience, Romantics assert, unless the unity and splendor of existence are powerfully apprehended by some powerful creative fusing in the human imagination. A very important part of Romantic literature is the drama of natural human tragedy—the finitude of the human consciousness in all of its failed aspiration and suffering agony.

But this is only the first phase of Hopkins' Romantic consciousness. There is a second phase that can be discerned in Romantic poets when operating at full creative capacity (Wordsworth's "Intimations" ode is a prime instance). The totally engaged Romantic imagination apprehends a deeper structure in Nature which reveals an awesome unity and harmony "deep down," an order that can be "seen" behind the individuality of the life of everything —the "unmediated vision." However, this perception requires a breakthrough imaginative consciousness in order to discover the stabilizing scale of Being and Thought and Word. Of course, the felt reactions to such a vision are almost inexpressible. The breakthrough to a second level of Nature is achieved by the imaginative intellect which penetrates the first level of individualized existence to some intimation of a common core in Nature. The breakthrough as a state of consciousness is a kind of psychic transport brought about by an unusual ordering of contemplative mental energy whose field of force both uplifts insight to the level of the visionary and deepens the feelings of rapport to levels of an assenting rapture permeating the entire experience. Nature and human nature coalesce into a rhapsodic, holistic state of comprehension (Coleridge's *Ancient Mariner* is an example). Such is the achievement of the total Romantic consciousness. M. H. Abrams called this Romantic state "natural supernaturalism."

The hallmark of Hopkins' Romanticism lies in his taking the transcendent level of Romantic consciousness to a point of a specific focus on Christ as the "core" of all Nature. Christ, in Hopkins' Romantic consciousness, "plays" in every individual existent in Nature, and thus everything is in some measure a personification of Him. Christ is "there" underneath the "Thereness" of Everything. To such an imaginative vision, all things in Nature are aspects of the Incarnation by virtue of which Presence the whole world is built and rebuilt to Christ's own mysterious but glorious purposes. This Christological notion, of course, was not original with Hopkins, nor was he the first to express it. Christo-centrism has a long tradition in Christianity from St. Augustine to Karl Rahner. What is original in Hopkins is his own poetic "inscaping" of his own breakthrough consciousness to a full-visioned Romantic Christian consciousness and his unique artistic expression of this marvelous dialectical flight. Also Hopkins is unique in that he placed the poetic legacy of Romanticism within the context of Christian belief, thereby restoring briefly the Christian legacy of Romanticism that began with Spenser and Milton. After the troubled assents and dissents of the prime English Romantics—Blake, Wordsworth, Coleridge, Byron, Shelley, and Keats—Hopkins was able to say through powerful religious poetry that the Christian Incarnation is indeed the divine reality within everything, that every just person "acts what in God's eye he is— / Christ." No major poet since Blake had said this with such deep poetic conviction. And his fusion of the Ignatian meditative method with

Scotus' philosophy in an attempt to found in imaginative reason a "new Realism" was a daring effort to establish a rationale for his Christian Romantic consciousness.

"As kingfishers catch fire, dragonflies draw flame," for example, exhibits the Romantic, Ignatian, and Scotian qualities which shaped the uses of Hopkins' religious imagination. The poem first of all reveals the Romantic sensibility experiencing directly Nature's "inscapes" in the most minute detail. Characteristically Hopkins' visual powers seized upon those facets which revealed to him signs of deep "instresses"—a natural and sacral dimension co-existent in the very beings of the things absorbed. Such experiential encounters in which the natural and the sacral are simultaneously comprehended are elemental in the high Romantic, poetic personality. The imaginative sensibility is somehow surcharged to a point of deep penetration into the essences of the things experienced. Out of this discovered deep structure arises the transporting visionary awareness which the creative imagination begins to make into symbolic orders. In this poem Hopkins began with very simple "scapes" yet they represent everything elementally as fire, water, earth, and air. The resultant transport, then, encompasses the whole range of being.

The Ignation aspect of the sonnet is evident in its triune structure. The Ignation poet composes the objects of his contemplation (birds, insects, rocks, and water, and bells) with rich perceptions into their selving patterns. This is followed by moral and philosophical considerations in which the poet reflects upon the significance of the "selving" in all Creation which brings him to an understanding of the principle of individuation in all things: every being has exactly the created nature God endowed it with—the out-wording of a divine in-wordness.

This understanding leads to the third episode of the Ignation meditation—the colloquy. This occurs in the sestet in which the poet applies his composition of Nature's "me-ing" and his intellective analysis of its significance of himself (human nature). The cast for the human "inscape" is God Himself and thus the poet is moved to speak of how "justice" requires human beings to choose that self-expression which best reflects the model God sent—Christ, the perfect God-man. This powerful recognition causes the poet to speak, to say in colloquy, how in modeling Christ—the just model—human nature takes on Christhood through grace, the most pleasing glory that can be given to God. The poet talks of how Christians assimilate Christ and thus assume His character, and because of this Christians "feature" Him in all of their own self-expressions. The colloquy reaches its close at the very end of the poem which concludes with a celebrating assent of "me-ness" as "Christness." The Ignatian meditative pattern is completed with the exclamation: "To the Father through the features of men's faces."

The poem also contains Hopkins' Scotian sense of "this-scapes" in the throngs of Nature's variety. Each thing in telling itself "words" Creatorship as the goodness of every individual thing making up the indivisible perfection of God. Hopkins in his Scotian visuality sees natural and manmade colors, sounds, and patterns as the dramatic "telling" of Creaturehood—the azured kingfisher, the jet flame of the dragonfly, the exchanges between stone and water, the bells tongueing their names—all finding their own true voices to say their own unique names. Each self-declaration at the same time is in fact a harmonizing part in the chorus of voices making up the great choir of Creation, each in singing its part (selfness) with all others making collectively the universal music of the Creator's masterpiece.

There is another Scotian emphasis in the poem. Hopkins accepted Scotus' idea that individuality is intrinsic to being prior to actual existence; thus existence brings out the individuality already there. The individuality of a being is a distinct intention in God's mind whether or not actual existence is ever conferred. Thus actual existence is God uttering Himself in this world about which Hopkins said in a note on *The Spiritual Exercises,* "the world, man, should after its own manner give God being in return for the being he has given it or should give him back that being he has given. This is done by the great sacrifice. To contribute then to that sacrifice is the end for which man is made. . . ." (*Sermons*, 129.) Sacrifice is what Hopkins meant by "the just man justices," the Scotian emphases being choosing to contribute to the Great Sacrifice through the self-expression of choice and desire: "Keeps grace: that keeps all his goings graces." Through such actions Christians become through the mystery of grace Christ—a selfness in self and a selfness in Christ—which constitutes a reverse Incarnation in which selfness is sent back to God, Christ-selving as a returned free act of love: "Lovely in limbs, and lovely in eyes not his, / To the Father through the features of men's faces."

The "kingfisher" sonnet is Romantic transport, Ignatian colloquy, and Scotian individuation combined through the powers of the sanctifying imagination into a wonderfully rich religious poem. The poem itself, of course, represents a unique selving of the Christian poet, Hopkins, who "acts . . . Christ" in the very making of the poem.

It is the drama of the spiritual take-off and flight of this stereoscopic consciousness that is the primary subject of the new religious poetry Hopkins wrote. The first instance of this kind of poem to emerge after "The Wreck" was "God's Grandeur."/60/ Interestingly, by happenstance, it is a precedent poem in Hopkins' canon in that it was written in the poetic form which Hopkins found to be the most organically related to his religious imagination—the sonnet. This poem announced the two thematic motifs which are to sound and resound throughout the rest of Hopkins' poetry—the "two natures" in all existence and the wondrous, difficult duty to apprehend this truth. In this one preamble poem, Hopkins stated what might serve as a pre-amble for *The Divine Comedy* and *Paradise Lost:* there is a divine subsidy in Nature in the person of Jesus Christ whose Presence is "seeable" and whose powers of renewing incarnations in the personhood of the Holy Spirit, Lord and giver of life, continually create and recreate the thousands of faces of Nature; the destiny of human consciousness is to know and love God in and through the incomparable transports of the human personality in the company of Nature's throng. The meaning is not new, but the song is. What makes Hopkins' poetry so powerful, so challenging, so dramatic, so startling, is not his restatement of the Christocentric meaning to existence; it is his unique, creative, poetic affirmation that God is knowable directly, experientially, really, by the marvelous means of the flights of the astronautical human consciousness. The crux of his poetry is the dramatization of the personal creativity of human powers in the act of discovering God in the reality of human consciousness, and the powerful symbolization of that fresh realization into new, original, poetic "scapes." A poetic act of this kind, then, is new being, thought, and word forged into an original imitation of the continuous creative presence of Christ in "the dearest freshness deep down things"; this momentous power of Nature is also "the dearest freshness deep down" the human person. Each in his own way, Blake, Wordsworth, and Yeats had talked about this "freshness" in his poetry; Hopkins is a member of their visionary company. In his poems/61/ "The Starlight Night," "Spring," "In the Valley of the Elwy," "Pied Beauty," "Hurrahing in Harvest," "The Lantern out of Doors," "As kingfishers catch fire," "The Leaden Echo and the Golden Echo," Hopkins dramatizes the flights of the astral Romantic consciousness probing to the landscape of Christian beatitude in all of its awesome transport, dazzling encounters, and joyous discoveries. The key to reading these poems is "The heart rears wings bold and bolder / And hurls for him, O half hurls earth for him off under his feet." Hopkins' poetic quest was to re-create Christ selving in Nature's diversity.

Such fabulous spiritual, poetic flights are dangerous as well as beautiful. Perhaps this is why the one poem among Hopkins' lyric poems of Romantic transport that has attracted the most attention is "The Windhover."/62/ More powerfully than all other sonnets, it casts the glorious vision of immortal beauty in mortal terms of common experience as well. The result is a poem which is the most concentrated poetic statement of the existential predicament of the Romantic Christian consciousness that Hopkins wrote. The sonnet's importance requires for our purposes another reading.

"The Windhover" has been critical fair game for a great number of readers of Hopkins. I have felt for some time that the deluge of interpretive analyses of this fine poem has been characterized so often by contrasting the contents of the religious experience in the poem to some analysis of esthetic form. Those readers who are unable to sympathize with the religious commitments in the poem are left with art for art's sake. However, Hopkins had no patience with make-believe esthetic experience.

"The Windhover" is about the incredible power and beauty of the drama of Christian contemplative energy, the very essence of Hopkins' Romantic imagination. The state of imaginative-religious consciousness that Hopkins describes in the sonnet can be used as a representation in poetic form of the epistemology of this "new Realism" whose aims, among other purposes, are to resist the reduction of experience and art to merely the dynamics of personality. Hopkins, of course, encountered this point of view in the person of its greatest expositor, Walter Pater. Experience for Pater, as we have noted previously, was mainly a matter of mind-flow with no satisfactorily real organizing principle outside the mind. For him art is a temporary record of experience. In Hopkins' view, Pater is only half-right. Mind-flow transience, yes, but the brittleness of experience arises from the finiteness of the perceiving personality. Despite this limitation, though, Hopkins asserts a center to things, to which a flow of awareness is clearly possible, "a history of growth, and mounts from the part to the whole." This element in the perceptions of consciousness signals a footing for reality, an organic process of knowledge, and a holding center in reality. As he put it in his "new Realism" notes about the father of Realism, Parmenides, "To be and to know or Being and thought are the same." This is another way of saying that Hopkins is a full Romantic and Pater is not. Despite their associations and some strong esthetic affinities, the gulf between them, intellectually and artistically, is unbridgeable.

Nowhere is this more significantly clear than in their ideals of artistic form. For Pater, the "esthetic word" is a kind of wand to waft the consciousness on flights of fancy and revery, whereas to Hopkins the "artistic word" is a way of acknowledging the essential unity that exists between the mind, reality, and language. This unity affirms an order and meaning outside the observer, hence a "realism" which the consciousness encounters and which the imagination expresses. To Hopkins, art separated from real principles of Being is an art separated from truth and life; like Ruskin he held that art reduced to its pure esthetic considerations is an expression of dying consciousness, an apparition that haunts all Paterian estheticism. Many readings of "The Windhover" are attempts to interpret the poem in Paterian terms, that is, in terms of the poet struggling with a negating religiousness. Such a reading forces a crack in the tone and form of the sonnet. These readings are generally marked by their strong tendencies to separate the vital connection the poet asserts in the poem between the falcon and Christ.

The falcon's flight in the sonnet, the starting place in the poem, is a poetic replica of a real existent that has its own separate "instress-inscape" apart from the "catching" consciousness of the poet. So first of all the poem is about "catching" the falcon. Applying to his Romantic mentality, Hopkins meant he "saw" the bird in the full plane of its own natural being; he "instressed" the falcon "inscape." To the true Romantic consciousness in the fullness of its contemplative-creative energies, the first plane of Nature generates a new "seeing," namely a witnessing in some way that the "Brute beauty and valour and act" of the natural bird is also a manifestation of an upper reality abiding in all the entities of Nature. The falcon then is double-natured, itself and what I have called "Christ-scape" "playing" in created Nature. But the deeper joy, as I believe is always the case in Hopkins' poetry, is the fabulous flight of consciousness to achieve and express this great insight to the "Hero" so present in the world. The poem is a great wonder because Hopkins has thrillingly caught the transcending dialectic of his poetic, visionary experience with powerful feelings, admiration, and exaltation. The poet had reached that level of beatific transport so that his catching of the bird became a "catching of Christ" featured in the bird. The poem is in part an "inscaping" of the poet's apprehension in his own experience of the glorious, mysterious union of Divinity, Nature and Humanity—all "buckled" in the dense structure of All-Being. Such is the witnessing of the center of Everything, a witnessing of which is awesome and overwhelming. This is the creative "fire" that breaks out between the observer and observed whose light and life claims the heart and mind. For poet and reader the poem is a charge from the creative energy generated in the Romantic creative consciousness whereby the enormous powers of the contemplating mind are put in action to re-create itself apprehending the flight of the falcon-Christ-imagination "riding" in the mystery of real existence. Being (divine and natural) and thought (vision) and word (poem) are "buckled" to a new, daring level of newly created "inscape," mirroring the grand "scape" of Being. The falcon in the poem becomes the poet-Christ and the "striding / High there" the bold flight of the Romantic consciousness achieving the "mastery of the thing!" The bird of Nature is the bird of the Christ-consciousness flying into the poet's imaginative religious consciousness.

Had Hopkins continued in this vein with celebratory words of adoration, petition, and salvation, as he did in "The Wreck," perhaps "The Windhover" would not have baffled so many readers, but he did not. Instead, Hopkins returns to ground level, so to speak, and reminds us of the hidden character of this mystical union of existence. The sestet returns to the common experience of mortal beauty but with a changed "visionary" perspective. Now every common thing is bathed in the beatific light of the "fire" that breaks from the transformed religious consciousness. Everything is changed; nothing is the same. We now know that the falcons of this world in all of their mortal beauties are also expressions of the immortal beauties of the selving of the glorious, radiant, Divine Dauphin soaring in his "daylight" kingdom, radiating His immortal beauty in all of its splendor in and through the world's natural beauty. How wonderful it is that the "fire that breaks" out from this visionary truth is also the energy that brings this transcendent meaning to the "catching" eye of the vision-seeker in the form of an illuminating creative power that lights up the superstructure of all existence. However, the immortal beauty "deep down" is fastened to surface mortal beauty; "Christ-scape" is plunged in "Nature-scape." Incarnationalism is not only the glorious mountaintops of beatific, visionary landscapes; Incarnationalism is also Divine Presence in dying natural and human forms. So while Christ plays in the human and natural beauties of this world, He also works-suffers in their mortal, natural fates. This is also a part of the splendid vision of the "buckle" of Everything, the dangerous part.

With amazing economy and simplicity, Hopkins shifts the focus of the contemplating mind from the splendor of the "Christ-scape" in Being to the "great sacrifice"/63/ implicit in the "scapes" of the Incarnation. The presence of Divinity in natural forms is a great, inspiring mystery when glimpsed as the "freshness deep down things," but an even greater and a more mysterious phenomenon when "caught" in the devolving, disintegrating death "deep down things." Because Hopkins expressed both aspects of the Incarnational vision, readers of the poem have been troubled. Yet within the "buckle" of Everything is both the heroic triumph of existence victorious in Christ and the humiliating death of Nature immolated in Christ. The last tercet of the poem completes the meditation on the Incarnation.

Of course, the contrast is jarring, even upsetting. And the poet is aware of its difficulty. He says, "Try not to marvel at what I am now going to say. That same mighty and powerful majesty of God I showed you present in that marvelous, chivalric-acting bird is also present in the common, ordinary things like plowing (birth and work) and fire (life and death). The same Christ-bird heroics are present in the sweat of our brows and in the 'breaking down' of everything. These are also 'scapes' of the Lord which come into the vision of the contemplating eye. So you see why my heart was so stirred. I had been trying to see Him during my days of daily bread through my 'plod' and 'dying embers' [Ember days are days of special fast and abstinence in the Catholic Church] when the glorified Christ suddenly burst forth triumphant, transcendent of the Sacrificed Christ. I know both 'Christs' are intrinsically present in all things, but it is so much rarer, so much more encouraging and affirming, to 'catch' the Christ of his bliss than to dig Him out of 'the stroke dealt.' I have come to know the Christ of the driven Passion, the Christ of change, failure, decay (prayer, sin, and death), the Christ of so much religious experience in this life. It is so much harder to 'catch' the 'lovely asunder Christ' of all Being, in daily thought, word, and deed. Yet I know, and do hereby acknowledge, that He is there, glorified in His sacrificed Presence and ready to be 'fetched in the storm of His strides.' " (In my paraphrase I have made use of passages from "The Wreck" in order to emphasize that the sestet of "The Windhover" is a miniature of Part the Second of the longer *Deutschland* ode.) In this great sonnet Hopkins again expressed the complete vision of his transported religious consciousness at a rare level of transcendent vision.

What is difficult in this poem for many readers, and justly so, is the grounding of the "falcon" Christ in the dust and ashes of the "sheer plod" Christ. Of course, there is no answer for this paradox except the mystery of the Incarnation (and by extension all Incarnationalism). Hopkins himself had difficulty. He was helped by Scotus who asserted that the heroic Christ entered the natural and human orders out of love, but this love became a sacrificed love. Ecstasy came first, said Scotus, then immolation. "The Windhover" is thrilling and uplifting as the drama of "catching" the ecstasy of the soaring divine presence rather than the laboring and burdened presence in the human and natural orders. However, the poet had to acknowledge what his experience had confirmed, what his spiritual mentors told him, that "buckled" to the "dapple-dawn-drawn Falcon" is the "sheer plod" and the "Fall, gall, and gash" of the Passion-scape of the Incarnation. The implications are frighteningly awesome, for, to make the point in Blakean terms, the Lamb and the Tiger are one, are us, are Everything, are "Christ-scapes." How can this be, and if so, how can such a truth be authenticated in our experience? No wonder readers, especially those who have no portals at the upper ends of their imaginative experiences, find all of this difficult. However, all readers stop in awe, silenced by reverence and admiration, or both.

For those who have an inkling of what Hopkins said in "The Windhover," there is only humbling awe. Clearly the poet had experienced some extraordinary moment of awareness in which he "caught" Christ as the Incarnation of heroic love and passion. He "caught" a Christ in but beyond experience, and from that transcendent sight he, for the nonce, "saw into the life of things." It is all too rare and inexplicable, the journeys of the Romantic religious consciousness and its fabulous tales. Hopkins considered "The Windhover" his best poem. Perhaps this was so because it "caught" the Romantic "scape" of the poet as no other poem did—"the achieve of, the mastery of" the "Falcon" imagination of the poet.

X

The poems Hopkins wrote as a priest form a distinctive group. Omitting incidental pieces like "The May Magnificat" which demonstrate the stark difference between pious poetry, the stock of religious verse (though Hopkins' is of a very high order), and the power pieces of a surcharged Romantic consciousness, and "The Loss of the Eurydice," an instance of Hopkins writing largely under the impulse of writing itself, the popularization of his style, readers can discern that the poems which Hopkins wrote from his ordination in 1877 to his posting in Ireland in 1884 have special kinship./64/ In them, Hopkins, the priest, confronts the arduous task of the Christian public ministry and experiences a deep sense of spiritual twilight and ruin both in Nature and human life. This harsh encounter brought forth an element in his poetry that had its origins deeply embedded in his character, namely his moral fiber, a quality that had undergone fundamental shaping and special applications under the spiritual tutelage of Ignatius and Scotus. This characteristic has received a good deal of attention by students of Hopkins' spirituality. The notion of the "elective will," the way Hopkins understood the moral imperatives of choosing to trace Christ in personal experience and follow out the implications of that discovery, is a central issue in his life and work.

While the notion of "election of Christ" is a central focus of Ignatian spirituality, "the daily bread" of living Christ is rooted in the specific detail of basic, Christian religious experience through which "election" is realized. Moral idealism in personal conduct must be brought into the area of religious consciousness; personal religious experience is fashioned and shaped for greater spiritual transcendence out of the moral battleground of personal choice and desire. I have already discussed elsewhere in my study of Ignatian spirituality Hopkins' unusual notion and exercise of these two human faculties of choice and desire, so that he tended to stress disproportionately the "elective" to the detriment of the "affective" will. The result of this emphasis is evident in the priestly poems: Hopkins dwelt often upon the world as fallen and people as sinners. His stressing the preservation of moral innocence caused his poetry to focus on the simple, the childlike, and the ignorant—a kind of pristine religious consciousness. Such attachments to personal moral idealism also caused him to dissociate himself from all of the defilements of Nature. Of course, as general moral and religious tendencies, these motivations do and should exist in all sincere Christian believers, and indeed, these qualities can be found in Hopkins' poetry from the beginning. However, now the priest-poet turned his mature Christian religious consciousness to an emphasis that is familiar, the Christianity of sin, death, and hell. In these poems Hopkins tells us the differences between the life of a priest in the public ministry and that of the seminarian where religious experience is primarily deeply personal, "out of the swing of the sea."

What do these vocational poems tell us about Hopkins' priestly religious experience? In general these poems give witness to the chasm that exists between personal religious experience as self-spiritualization and the public profession of religious faith. How could a priest create public religious experience for his congregation that possessed the meaning and beauty of the personalized Romantic consciousness of the seminarian-poet? The answer to this vital question begins to come clear in the priestly poems, the first segment of which were written during Hopkins' extended assignment at Oxford. In these poems there are signs of a growing awareness in Hopkins of a difficulty which had catastrophic implications for him, namely, that his powerful Romantic consciousness expressed in original poetic forms had little or no part in his life as a public minister of Christ. The outward signs were ominous enough. "The Wreck" had been rejected, and he had not received any kind of vocational encouragement to make his poetic gifts a significant part of his priestly life in the Society of Jesus. He received no other encouragement as a priest-scholar. If indeed he had found the basis for a Christian Romantic synthesis (of course, he would not have described his notions in these terms), in his union of the theology of Scotus and the psychology of Ignatian meditation, there seemed no opportunity to fully develop his thinking in some scholarly forum. The Romantic poet and scholar seemed entirely apart from the Jesuit priest. How could his powerful Romantic nature with its strong intellectuality find fruitful realization in his life as priest?

The Oxford poems of 1878-79 tell of this struggle. Within the group the poems divide between those that express the Romantic consciousness "inscaping" Hopkins' own religious experience and those poems that seek correlative transport in his priestly experience. While it would be expected that personal religious experience would be richer than its enactment in public ministry, the relationship between the two seems to have been more unbalanced than usual. No doubt he sought earnestly the transported spiritual realization of his priesthood but with limited success. He seemed unable to relate his soaring, visionary religious consciousness to the reality of religion in the workaday world of the parish church. This failure increased into a burden which got heavier every day of his life. And the failure seeped into his private spiritual affections spoiling frequently the Christian bliss he saw and felt in Nature. More and more he begins to dwell upon the "strokes dealt" in Nature and the human consequences.

Take "Binsey Poplars,"/65/ for instance. In this poem, Hopkins' Romantic spirit is powerfully apparent in his great feelings of tenderness over touching or altering the natural organic order. However, behind his sense of ruined "scapes"

there is some deep unsettlement about some radical disharmony between Nature and humankind. Given his philosophy
of Being, ecological change might be seen as the emergence
of new and different forms co-created by humans into new
"self-scapes," new nature "poems." This was not the case;
rather more and more he felt such actions an intrusion into
the natural order, intrusions that were often seen as ecological tragedy brought on by "Ten or twelve, only ten or
twelve / Strokes of havoc unselve. . . ." Passages like this
suggest that the structure of his religious tranquility had
unbalanced so that the Holy Spirit no longer seemed to be
regenerating the world. Nature appeared to him to be
spoiled and despoiled to levels that amounted to naked
losses in Being with no intimations of any supernal
reprieve. Similarly human nature experienced the same
sense of radical existential insult in human death which he
expressed later in "Spring and Fall." The "blight man was
born for" increasingly beclouded his priestly religious
vision. A like kind of spiritual obtuseness is expressed in
poems like "The Candle Indoors," where he asks "What
hinders?" in the human heart's inability to reach beyond the
experience of life and nature's "fading fire." He felt
stymied: "I plod wondering, a-wanting, just for lack / Of
Answer," in trying to transfigure the religious experience of
his flock through the spiritual ministrations of his priesthood.

Naturally priestly religious transformation seems more
possible with the innocent. Hopkins, the priest, deeply felt
the richness of a child's faith. In "The Handsome
Heart,"/66/ a child gives a gracious answer and sweet
submission; Hopkins again felt the transport of "homing
nature . . . wild and self-instressed." And in "The Bugler's
First Communion"/67/ he expresses some spiritual self-
realization in his exercising his priestly vocation in
spiritually arming the young knight of Christ, "Christ's own
Galahad." This poem, perhaps, is the only poem in this
priestly group in which Hopkins expressed a felt fusion of his
full Romantic Christian consciousness and his priesthood in
strongly positive perspectives.

More typically he was thrown back from his priestly frustrations to his private, personal, religious consciousness to brood over his priestly difficulties (his failure as a preacher, for example), to stay his own spiritual heart (his scruples about publishing his poetry, a major moral dilemma), to explore the possibility of fresh applications of his poetic religious feelings, sometimes to celebrate the vitality of his own hidden heart "catching" God's grandeur. "Duns Scotus' Oxford"/68/ and "Henry Purcell"/69/ are such poems of this latter category, each possessing that rich sense of "instress and inscape" generated by the religious imagination entirely surcharged by penetrating the beauty of thought and art of each subject to a revelatory point of a felt transport. The resulting transcendent contemplative state of peaceful absorption and fulfilling contentment in the "scapes" of these two creative spirits freshly "inscaped" his own poetic mind—"but meaning motion fans fresh our wits with wonder" and "sways my spirits to peace." These are precious moments for "that piecemeal peace is a poor peace" that too often "come[s] to brood and sit," as he noted in "Peace."

The Christian poet dreamed perfection flowering in pristine Nature and human innocence, but the priest-poet felt plunged in a holy war with the fallen world. And his phalanx, the Church, in whose ranks he had enlisted to fight the good fight, seemed to be in a stalemate with the flesh and the devil. In his poem "Andromeda"/70/ Hopkins depicts his Church as nearly overwrought by her enemies. Christ, her Captain, conqueror of sin and death ("Gorgon's gear"), he says, will come when "no one dreams" and vanquish His Church's enemies ("fangs") by cutting her bonds ("thongs"). But in the meantime "Her Perseus" lingers, "Pillowly air he treads a time and hang, / His thought on her. . . ." The troops are left standing and waiting.

Soldiers in such a battle stance have as their greatest enemy the attrition of their militant will. Hopkins found in the lingering of Christ a lesson—to stand fast, to fight skirmishes, and to stand ready for the major engagement. In such lists the beauty in things dimmed at times and the deeper lights of transfigured sight darkened. With the spiritual background in shadows, the mundane stood out in the foreground of experience all the more menacingly. Natural and moral ugliness begloomed his senses. To a Christian Romantic as energized and militant as Hopkins was, "will power" loomed even more necessary.

The forging of Romanticism and Christianity in Hopkins' poetic personality was already in an alien relationship to the "fallen" world. His artistic metier was to soar, not to sour. Hopkins concentrated even more upon an Edenic idealization of human consciousness in his contemplation of the ways of the world. Thus the aboriginal calamity in creation and mankind became harder to accept.

Hopkins clearly found it more difficult to acknowledge the morally dreadful, the naturally evil mingled in the "scapes" of existence. Of course, moral doom and gloom had always been there; he had acknowledged them: "Generations have trod . . . / And all is seared with trade. . . ." But now the evil "distress" in things came into fresh focus. Why? He had at hand the Christian account of history, and the promises of Christ. Was this orientation not sufficient to sustain his faith and hope? It is possible that his moral and esthetic alarm arose from the way he conceived of the personal implications of Original Sin. For Hopkins, the battle of battles of this world is a personal struggle with evil. The real issue is the individual will as the pitch of personality "selving goodness." The "Fall" in history comes down to the psychology of will power in every chooser.

This concentration upon choices had complicated his religious mind very early on. In his school essay for Walter Pater entitled "The Origin of Our Moral Ideas," he asserts that *"there are two (in the broad sense) logics putting stress on the mind, one belongs to virtue, one to vice. . . ."*/71/ But what motivates the choice of virtue over vice? Is there a moral logic which compels the choosing of good and the avoiding of evil? Hopkins answers yes. After an analysis of three kinds of moral act as a movement of innate ideas in the mind, a socially motivated choice (Utilitarianism), and a sequence of acculturated value systems, Hopkins dismisses all three types of choice. In their stead he proposes that the origin of moral ideas lies in the integration of the personality, the human desire for a sense of personal unity. There is a compelling logic which moves us to virtue, Hopkins argues, and that force is a drive for a self-control that regularly harmonizes our options into some order that we perceive as self-perfection. As is often his habit, Hopkins uses art and the personality to make his point. His argument is telling because he must have known that his tutor, Pater, had identified the good with the beautiful, thereby making the origin of moral ideas the esthetic mind motivated by beauty. However Hopkins denies this. Rather he argues, while both art and ethics are systems of morality, they differ in their powers of personal fulfillment. While both integrate the human personality, each does it differently. Art brings about personal unity, but it is a secondary realization of the objective will. The first self-realization we seek is pure unity. Art is an impure unity because it works through difference. The origin of our moral ideas lies in our quest for "perfect realization, in perfect consistency." The logic of morality, then, is "the highest consistency in the highest excellence." It follows as a moral system, choosing is of a higher order than making, the affective will is secondary to the elective will. Why do we desire this higher order of the pure moral ideal? Hopkins' answer is the perfection of self-unity which is our only means of recognizing successfully our being to ourselves, unifies us, "while vice destroys the sense of being by dissipating thought . . . wickedness breaks up the unity of principle."/72/

We now have the key to Hopkins' difficulty to fit his Christian Romanticism with the world, the flesh, and the devil. Spiritual transport in religious experience depends upon loving (affective will), but loving is more than desiring. It is choosing (elective will) to make love possible. This ideal of psycho-moral harmony pervades Hopkins' Christian Romantic poetry. More and more, however, he began to stress the "elective" will at odds with the "affective" will. Unfortunately, this emphasis increased until it became a distortion of the reconciling interplay between choice and desire in his personality. There occurred in him a psychic disequilibrium between the logic of the unity of moral perfection and the unity of esthetic perfection. His moral conscience began to fight his Romantic consciousness.

After his Oxford undergraduate days, Hopkins had received, during his Jesuit training, further affirmation of his moral attitudes when he studied Scotus' theory of human personality. No doubt he sought enlightenment concerning the battle of wills in him because he quite rightly saw that the issue had great doctrinal as well as pastoral meaning. Viewed abstractly as theology, the question is: What are the differences between faith, morality and religion? The answers lay in an assessment of the arraying of the "elective" and the "affective" powers of the human personality, the structuring of the human soul. How can knowledge be deliberately united with love? In Scotus Hopkins found an acceptable answer to the harmonizing of the two "logics" in the human consciousness, an answer that Ignatius presumed in the practice of spiritual meditation. That answer is that human choice must be united with human desire to achieve total love. We must choose the good in order to love it. This is Scotus' attitude in his account of the powers of the human soul. Hopkins' own understanding of Scotus has been authoritatively studied and commented upon elsewhere./73/ However, for our purposes, the issue is not what Scotus explained or Ignatius assumed. Rather the problem is Hopkins' personal struggle to realize in himself a harmony of choice and desire, a union of his "affective" and "elective" wills, a fusing of art and morality.

Distinctions are important in understanding this difficulty in Hopkins. The problem did not arise because he became a Catholic or a Jesuit priest. The reconciliation between good acts and loving motivations is an elemental human struggle. Religion simply places the strife within new perimeters while the Christian religion structures choice and desire upon particular assents and affects, the center of which is the Incarnation of Christ. In Hopkins' case, there is no question of religious infidelity, nor is there any disengagement from his priestly vocation. Those commentators who have read the "terrible sonnets" as reflections of a frightful battle against religious doubt or vocational steadfastness are seriously mistaken (John Robinson and Daniel Harris are recent instances). What Hopkins was facing was and is what every sincere Christian believer and practitioner must face—to feel deeply about choosing to follow the values and ideals which Jesus put forth as the true way to human fulfillment. The more one aspires to imitate Christ in this sense, the greater the difficulty to achieve a Christian harmony of personal choice and desire. Any understanding of Hopkins' handling of this problem must begin with the fact that his religious aspirations were of the highest order; any discussion of his religious life must be carried on within this context.

Hopkins, then, like any other Christian (or any person who seeks to choose the good lovingly, for that matter, since religion is in the very soul of human perfection as a natural condition) knew the chasm between assenting to Christian beliefs and rejoicing in their personal realization. "Love thy neighbor," Jesus exhorted, which Christians universally accept as a basic belief in personal life, yet founder in its realization. Every Christian fights this good fight amid many losses and, indeed, it is part of the Christian faith that no Christian can truly close the gap between faith and works without God's personal help.

John Robinson suggests that Hopkins singularly failed to interiorize his Christianity with the result that he was unable, at least as a poet, to express Christian charity for his fellow human beings./74/ Robinson is touching a major topic in Hopkins' artistry, but I believe he has got it wrong. The origin of Robinson's view lies in his reading of the deep tension that surely exists in Hopkins' poetry beginning with the Oxford period and lasting until the final poems in Ireland. Robinson sees this tension as a failed interiorization of Christianity caused by Hopkins' "acutely developed aesthetic sense."/75/ In this understanding, Hopkins' religion was cut off by his art because art dwells on natural beauty but Christianity (religion) dwells upon ugliness (natural and moral evil). The result for Hopkins, according to Robinson, was a warping of his view of human nature and an "oscillation" between his loving and contemning human life. Another way of putting this is that Hopkins dwelt too much upon the logic of sin.

I agree with Robinson that there is a shift in focus in Hopkins' religious imagination and hence a change in his poetic style./76/ In his early religious poems, there is an enormous engagement with experiencing natural beauty, what he called "mortal beauty," as a gateway to preserve innocence, affirm Christian love, and to realize a sense of deep, personal spiritual harmony. It is not true to say that in these poems Hopkins seems oblivious of the disorganizing and disharmonizing elements in experience, for example, in "The Windhover." In these poems he emphasizes what I have called the Christian Romantic union of thought, being, and word, my way of expressing what Ignatius called "obedience of understanding," what Scotus examined as the diplomacy of choice and desire, what Hopkins himself discussed as the harmony of the "elective" and the "affective" wills. In these poems of Christian consolation, Hopkins' religious imagination has achieved a stable relationship with his religious reason. Somehow the "highest consistency" of his moral life was blended with the diverse unity of art. Esthetic unity seemed supportive of moral unity. Why this grace at this time, we shall never fully know. Hopkins certainly felt somewhat less the gap between law and love; certainly he was more reconciled to the existence of such a gap. He wrote in his Pater essay on moral ideals, ". . . in moral action our utmost efforts never result in its perfect realization, in perfect consistency."

What caused the unbalancing from a sense of interior unity between personal religious experience and the religious imagination? The answer, I believe, again lies in Hopkins' Christian Romantic state of mind. As we have seen, from his college days on he worked to blend two very strong tendencies in his nature. One was his enormously refined affective side that plunged him into his experiences of Nature with a very great richness of awareness, and a very powerful abstractive bent, which charged him to attempt to regularize observations upon some systemic principle. These personal forces, as I have attempted to show, caused him to seek in the history of thought some synthesis that would summarize and unify the knowledge continuum, that which evolved from the ground up (art) and that which organized experience from the top down (reason). To mention the most notable, he tried to fit Parmenides, Suarez, Ignatius, and Scotus into some kind of new synthesis. However, he got no further than a philosophical scaffolding. Time and opportunity for sustained construction seemed to have eluded him. The architecture of his synthesis remained a blueprint. Meanwhile he had to go on living his hypothesis, camped out on the building site, as it were. Confronting himself as a poet and as a priest, more and more the voluntarist emphasis began to take over his consciousness. Choosing rather than loving began to dominate his religious consciousness, perhaps because his affections were leading him off to less than his highest moral and religious ideals. The result was a risking of a deep alienation between the "elective" and the "affective" sides of his nature. The priest began to chastise the poet.

There are great dangers to the personality in such a situation. Health, harmony, and personal unity lie in loving what one chooses and taking the right choice through the great magnetic powers of desire. It is choosing desirable choices that satisfies our elective-affective human powers. The predicament of regularly forcing one side of one's nature to desire what appear to be undesirable choices is to enter into internal warfare of a most disintegrating kind. In Hopkins' case, it must be emphasized that the leading characteristic of his personality was Romantic, that is to say, imaginative, affective, phenomenologically sensuous. In such a personality, the affections take the strong lead in transporting outer experience to inner experience, transforming the mind from its outer side to its inner side. In such personalities, choice melts before the splendid beauties of visionary experience. Take Hopkins' "Pied Beauty,"/77/ for example. The poem is a catalogue of sense pleasure. As the poet's imaginative eye roves the world, the affective intensity of the poem gathers until it spills over from the natural world to the manmade, and grows to an omnium-gatherum. The affections have been gently led to greater and greater intensity, and when this enriched awareness reaches the point of felt realization of the source of all this goodness and beauty, the "elective" will has been moved from the opening, routine, ejaculatory adoration to a union of desire and choice, a state of integrated consciousness,

"Praise him," the ideal of human wholeness; as Hopkins wrote in his college essay, "our only means of recognizing successfully our being to ourselves, it unifies ourselves. . . ."/78/

What brought Hopkins to this divided personal state? I do not think it was any excessive esthetic attachment to the beauties of the natural world. From the beginning he saw the existential finitude in mortal beauty. It was not his personal inability to "live" his Catholic faith. He abided the paradox of innocence and sin that is the religious awareness of the Christian consciousness. After all, he had himself, as do all Christians, a firsthand experience of personal sin. Were the causes more external? Was it tied into his growing awareness that his peculiar talents were not finding a fully useful place in the Jesuit Society? Did this frustration produce a serious conflict between his own personality and the priestly life he seemed forced to live in the Society? Could it be that his undue stress on the "elective" side of virtue and goodness arose from his inability to bring any of his religious, academic, or artistic projects to completion and recognition? Where does his often precarious health fit in? Finally, more mysteriously, was the suffering and tepidness that gradually filtered into his spiritual notes God's way of calling him to higher personal holiness?

The answers to these questions can foster a number of speculations that have some validity. I see a very evident tendency in the poetry written after his Oxford assignment until his dispatch to Ireland of a cleavage between his Romantic-affective side and his Voluntarist-elective side. Whatever his intellectual grasp of the normal state of human consolation and personal unity born of an identification of choice and desire, Hopkins found it more and more difficult to feel his religious convictions. Just why this occurred will always remain an enigma in his personality.

XI

Before tracing in some detail Hopkins' later poetry this opposition in his voluntary nature, there are some caveats to be considered. First, every human being regularly and continually faces the psycho-moral predicament of achieving internal harmony of choice and desire. So what Hopkins endured was the perennial human condition, though in his case somewhat exacerbated. Second, all his mentors generally emphasized the health and holiness of choosing what we love. Third, in our desires we often mistake true good for apparent good and, in doing so, frequently bring to bear upon our "elective" natures the same spontaneous flow of feeling that emanates from the appetency of true good. In such cases, the "elective" will must fight off the allures of vagrant desires and must attempt to restore the integrity of desire. Fourth, at times the "elective" will can choose to offend the sensuous mind by contrarily denying legitimate desire through misdirected discipline or idealism. The result is a state of internal warfare in which the "elective" powers act punitively so that feelings are chastised, clamped down, "swallowed." These paradigms of the human voluntary powers are part of the drama of human personality as Hopkins' mentors had depicted disconsolation. Hopkins suffered them all in the normal human way.

The disconsolation in Hopkins' poetic and religious mind is quite evident in his letters, papers and poetry. Early on, Hopkins felt this loss of transport, and tried to firm up his "elective" will. The struggle is expressed with poetic power in his poem "As kingfishers."/79/ The sonnet declares the consoling transport of his original Christian Romanticism in the usual mode of Ignatius and rationale of Scotus, but in addition there is in the poem a heavy focus upon selving as moral activity: *"What I do is me: for that I came."* In the sestet he asserts that, unlike the rest of existence, human selving is more of a process of election than affection: "the just man justices...." This difference is fully compatible with the transcendent affirmation he had achieved in his religious imagination—the "Christ-scape" is the deep spiritual structure of all selves and selving—still the analogy of kingfishers, dragonflies, stones, and bells spontaneously "tell" themselves in their own natural ways while the unity of being in human persons requires a different "dealing" out of self. Here the poet's simile, unlike surrounding poems, is strained by his emphasis upon the "elective" will justicing, keeping grace more by some naked determination than by a heart-stirring spiritual transport beyond natural experience, where the transcendent, awesome beauty of Christ so floods the "affective" will that the "elective" will surrenders to the beautiful as truly good. I am not suggesting that Hopkins' poetical-religious-moral universe is breaking down. Rather the dynamic seems to have moved from a Christian and Romantic (affective) spirituality to a Voluntarist, Christian (elective) spirituality. Apologists contrarily will, of course, argue that this emphasis has been always present in Hopkins as a necessity to his continuous religious development. This position is sound, yet the human self dealt out in the poem can be read as an opposing self "crying" out its poor "thisness," while non-human nature naturally catches fire, draws flame, rings, flings out its being-self. There was always a moral imperative at the heart of Hopkins' Christian Romantic experience which can be found in his exuberant exhortations to respond to the "flaming" spiritual beauty in the deep structure of experience. Now, however, the moral logic surfaces from some absolutist drive which seems to be forcing itself upon experience from the outside. This tendency increases in Hopkins' poetry resulting in poems which are dramatizations of the psychomachia of the two warring "logics" going on inside of him—choosing and loving the "Christ-scape."

This unbalancing spiritual consciousness is apparent even in the pure nature poems. "Inversnaid," for example, dwells upon its "darksome" aspects, and in "Ribblesdale"/80/ he speaks of the vulnerability of Nature and "dear and dogged" man's powerless elective plight to see the connections between mortal and immortal beauty. Here the poet projects his feelings as the earth's "care and dear concern."

Moreover, ordinary persons are mostly unaware of the dilemma of mortal beauty. Looking into a "great shadowy barn," Hopkins recorded in his notebooks, "I thought how sadly beauty of inscape was unknown and buried away from simple people and yet how near at hand if they had eye to see it and it could be called out everywhere again."/81/ How different from the vigilant calls to see and hurrah "Christ-scape" out of everything. In "Felix Randall," for example, while there is much priestly compassion for the farrier (Hopkins actually administered to the man who is the subject of this poem) the reader feels the priest's sense of helplessness more than his consolation. There he was, the poet tells us, one day "big-boned and hardy-handsome," and the next "sickness broke." Seeping through the poet's feelings of tender priestly ministrations of the sacrament of last rites are the shudders of sudden and absolute blight of human mortal beauty—". . . child, Felix, poor Felix Randall."/82/ The religious imagination is not soaring; it is sinking. Moreover the priest's ministrations have slipped away.

Accompanying this deeply felt awareness of twilight and ruin in things is a sense of responsibility. A new emphasis in this group of Hopkins' poems in the 1880s is his increasing feeling of sin and guilt. It is true that all of Hopkins' life has a remarkable moral earnestness about it, a quality that abounds in all his utterance. Indeed no Romantic poet ever felt the pull to connect transcendent spirituality to conduct as did Hopkins. His deep choices, even at a very tender age, were always bent toward fulfilling a deep asceticism in his personality, whatever his desires. He did not have to read St. Ignatius to discover how to use all things to the greater glory of God, though, of course, Ignatius' seconding of this penchant in him had its effect as a powerful reinforcement. Reading "Spelt from Sibyl's Leaves" in conjunction with "To what serves Mortal Beauty?" and "The Leaden Echo and the Golden Echo"/83/ reveals the spectrum of contending spiritual forces impacting his religious imagination. In the first two poems, Hopkins expresses a newly felt Paterian sensitivity to the fleetingness of human experience, a freshly dealt awareness of a perpetual motion to oblivion in all natural things, unless arrested momentarily in some way. Even the slowed time of expressive art forms allows the consciousness to taste only briefly the fruit of the experience. But then there must be the letting go, for no mortal beauty can be kept back. A darkness at the center of things blots all out into "disremembering." The poet seems to have felt a kind of Hegelian determinism or a Calvinist predestination as the encompassing fate of everything, especially humanity which will

81

be overwhelmed in the "whelm" of dark death. This view of humankind caught in the cracks of the earth's unraveling has a Hellenic tragic quality both in its cosmic universality as well in the wareness of a titanic struggle between huge forces of good and evil. Each person's moral conduct is a facet of this world battle, and so every personal action is part of this colossal tangle. Personal fate is shrouded in some deeper, unfathomable power which will determine the outcome, good or evil, once and for all, unless some "election" is made for rescue. In these poems, readers feel a deep anxiety of being trapped in the middle of a Gordian moral muddle as people, full of destined agony, unstring themselves, at times witlessly, on the right or wrong side of moral order. The priest ministering to an indifferent world such as this, going its own hellbent way, comes through very powerfully.

This shift in Hopkins from a heightened sense of Christ "scaping" the world before his very eyes to a sense of the world afflicted, turned loose, lurching out of its center to some Armageddon, is not a new religious awareness in Hopkins, but at this time in his life it is a surprising new emphasis. Fr. C. Devlin has discussed the pertinent biographical details occasioning Hopkins' depression/84/ and, more recently, Daniel Harris has suggested the dangerous lapses into "pathetic fallacy" such an apocalypticism is heir to. The period of religious feelings of transcendence seemed to have dimmed. In 1882 he urged, "Give beauty back," but some three years later, this generous election seems to have lost some of its transfiguring effect. Now his religious experience is associated with the "rack"—"thoughts against thoughts in groans grind."

The rich, uplifting awareness of his transported religious experience wherein he could reach out "yonder" dissipates. He felt himself become like those lamented ones for whom the "inscapes" of this world are "unknown and buried." This change in his religious experience is not mysterious or unknown. Annals of Christian aspirations are filled with such accounts of the accedia which Hopkins called "world sorrow." Moreover, we know some of the biographical reasons why Hopkins felt disappointed, frustrated, and sterile. What is interesting and important to us here is the impact of such desolating religious experience on Hopkins' religious imagination. Did Hopkins let his poetry slip into a Paterian impressionism in which his imagination seesaws in a mass of fleeting sensation achieving only momentary shapes whose centers continually cave in? Did the poet let himself sink down into that phantom psychic world of the self in which the imagination wanders through a nightmare journey, full of confusion and alarm? Did Hopkins, the Romantic, fall into that lower Romantic consciousness of self-pity, lamentation, alienation, and desolation?

There is no doubt that Hopkins' Romantic consciousness underwent some significant changes. One piece of evidence of this is his sonnet "To what serves Mortal Beauty?,"/85/ the last poem in his canon before the "terrible sonnets." This poem is a kind of preamble to this great personal crisis in his life. This crisis was made up of many elements. No doubt Hopkins had, during his tertian year (a period of vocational review and reaffirmation) leading up to his making his Last Vows to live as a Jesuit, come to grips with his own career as a priest. He knew himself well enough to know that ordinary pastoral service was not his strength, nor was teaching. He had brought to the Society three powerful personal strains: a dominating drive to live the ascetic life, an enormous expressive creativity along with a deep intellectual acuity that ranged widely in the areas of religion, esthetics, and literature. But to exercise these extraordinary talents within the milieu of the Jesuit priesthood, Hopkins needed supporting circumstances, promising opportunities; more especially, he needed some license from his superiors to foster in him those conducive motivations that energize the intellectual and creative life. After his tertianship, he saw clearly that those underwriting supports necessary for his creative urges were not likely to be available, and so he was left to fend for himself as best he could. He began to see that his hopes for a "new Realism" might never be formally formulated, that the productions of his Christian Romantic consciousness would never be acknowledged, that all might be left, as he said later, "a lonely began."

Could he go on at least in his now life-long secluded way producing for the shelf? Would his religious imagination soar anyway? His poem "To what serves Mortal Beauty?" gives us his answer. He was not being moved to experience that spiritualizing transcendence brought on by his transporting religious imagination as he had before this time. His high Romantic consciousness had been altered. How could he function creatively without seeing generating "Christ-scapes" at the center of his experience? Had his imaginative graces been reduced to a play of senses seeking some esthetic form to hold them momentarily in some especially delightful pattern before all crumbled again into a common jumble? Previously his religious imagination revealed clearly the purpose of mortal beauty: "Mortal Beauty" half "hurled" him into Christ's orbit. Now he felt grounded. He began to have religious feelings of a kind of spiritual quarantine at a secular level of consciousness. In 2 Cor. 7:10, Paul wrote, ". . . the sorrow of the world worketh death."

As he experienced this creative-religious strike, did he think of Walter Pater, his Oxford master, who said all experience is relative, that the great task of life is to purify the great mass of fleeting fragments of sense files to some point of esthetic unity? Did it all come down to the subjective powers of personality shaping patterns into impermanent forms? Pater had settled for the principle of esthetic form as the only deep order in things; Hopkins rejected this by insisting on a deific form as the central structure in being. He was now freshly confronted in the most personal terms with Pater's alternative in the dilemma of the "absolute" and the "relative" in experience. His "new Realism" seemed to be cracking and his creative, high Romantic consciousness fleeting.

All of these questions are implicit in the question Hopkins asks in opening the poem, "To what serves mortal beauty—dangerous; does set danc- / ing blood—the O-seal-that-so feature, flung prouder form / Than Purcell tune lets tread to?" It is as if Hopkins, under new pressures to accede to Pater's answer, denies him again. He answers that Beauty keeps us in touch with reality and may by grace open up an insight of some spiritual consequence. Something like this must have happened to Pope Gregory when he saw the mortal beauty of the Angles in the Roman slave market, which inspired him to send Augustine to Christianize Britain. The poet says that God stroked through beauty that day. So much it be with all mortal beauty. We must "instress" the "scapes" of the natural world lovingly, especially human beauty, mortal beauty in its highest form, but then stand back and wish for God's stroke to immortalize it. Hopkins allows for no Paterian esthetic revery; he calls for selfless recognition that the "scapes" of this world are "God-scapes." The poet affirms a Divine center to everything even if the stroke of "Christ-scape" is not manifested, not felt, incommunicable.

This was to be Hopkins' answer to the loss of spiritual power in his religious imagination. The poet of great religious transport does seem to back off, does acknowledge that something has changed in his religious imagination which has curtailed its expressive, visionary flights in "scaping" the deeper forms in things. Perhaps he was acknowledging that his Ignatian meditative exercises had lost some of their spiritualizing powers and that his Scotistic intuition had gone dead. He seems to have felt some spiritual disconnection about which he could do nothing except endure. Still he was hanging on. He would meet Mortal Beauty, and he would remain hopeful that "God's better beauty, grace," would greet him there. The hanging on, however, proved neither easily said nor done.

XII

The darkness that descended upon Hopkins in the last years of his life was different from earlier periods of tepidness. We know some of the external sources of his bad news. Foremost among his disconsolations was his deep sense of failure as a Jesuit priest. His scholarship, preaching, teaching, poetry, all seemed to him a "lonely began," as he put it. Surely his work was not as fruitless as he at times felt it to be. Perhaps what cast a dark spell over his life's work was his failure to convert even those closest to him to the Catholic faith, neither family nor friends. On top of these disappointments came his posting to Ireland in 1884 to teach in a makeshift university, itself the result of unsuccess. This posting seemed to him a kind of descent into hell, for Ireland was full of seething hatred and blind bitterness over Home Rule. Hopkins, a strong patriot but an honest one, was grieved on all sides by the political questions tearing England and Ireland apart. The times were fearsome, he believed, because England had betrayed the true faith, was becoming in fact less Christian every day. All of this put Hopkins into a new weariness about the emptiness of the times, a weariness which seeped down far into his consciousness. He was never to regain for any extended period his "fine delight."

"To seem the stranger"/86/ is about Hopkins' feelings about being in Ireland. His letters and journal tell us how difficult this assignment was for him. Ireland in the 1880s was a very unpleasant place for a British Jesuit to be posted, and Hopkins' assignment to a foundering university only added to a deep sense of displacement. Reading this sonnet one feels a sense of the imprisoning solitude which Hopkins expressed in the poem, almost as if he had been put in "solitary confinement" for misconduct. The poem tells of a kind of personal bafflement in the poet's life compounded of feelings of alienation, exile, strangeness, loneliness, and, most especially, spiritual aridness. The "underthought" in the sonnet is an inconsolable sadness which has reduced the spirit to only lost starts at stirring itself to do something. Is the sense of defeat and abandonment told of in the poem the result of some secret failure or misconduct? The poem gives no indication of moral justice being carried out; rather the temper of the sonnet is one of quiet painfulness in which the wounded lie suffering on the battlefield during a lull in the hostilities. Yet this "jack, joke, poor potsherd" does not set his sins against such treatment, does not rage at being left to this alien struggle for his life, does not condemn in bitterness. Hopkins does not question why he should be bereft of his home-centered "inscapes" of the Incarnation in his priestly and poetic life. He does not say God has jilted him and worse, has thrown him down on his own bitter failures. Rather he endures "heaven's baffling ban," but not without tears. In such dire circumstances the strain between the "affective" and "elective" will is very great when all that is desirable confronts one's harsh choices.

What is different about this last period of Hopkins' poetic career is that his personal experience caused him to produce a new kind of religious poem. I think this happened because his descent into spiritual depths this time went beyond disconsolation into outright desolation. Hopkins was forced for the first time to undergo religious experience which did not have the saving natural "graces" of mortal beauty, creativity, professional work, and friendship. Heretofore, one or more of these activities were grace-carriers which lifted him back to the balance of consolation and very often to personal, spiritual and artistic ecstasy. He felt help originating within and beyond himself, loving and caring he didn't deserve, which filled him with the joy of the "incomprehensible certainty." Now for really the first extended time, he was faced with the religious experience of spiritual desolation. The graces he groped for were very different and when deliverance came, the bestowal altered his religious consciousness and hence his religious imagination.

I wish to be very clear about my reading of this period of Hopkins' religious and poetic career. Unlike many other interpreters, I am asserting that what Hopkins was experiencing, though unusual, was a different kind of religious experience which changed the enablements of grace available to him. The old patterns of renewal and avowal seemed to no avail. There is no question here of slipping out of Ignatian spiritual mentorship; Ignatius knew of religious disconsolation and offered advice in his *Spiritual Exercises* for dealing with it. There is no weakening of Hopkins' faith commitment at all, for there is not a shred of evidence that he was experiencing any serious religious doubts. Nor is there any retreat whatsoever from his vocation as a priest or his life as a member of the Society of Jesus, whatever his difficulties. Finally, within the context of Christian spirituality, there is no basis to warrant talk about "God withdrawing" simply because in the recordings of such religious experiences, it is overwhelmingly manifest that God is felt to be present as in no other religious experience, so intensely that one's own self goes into a shock of recognition of the divine–human encounter. Fear and trembling abound, the self shakes, and the spiritual integrity of one's very own being is at stake. God becomes incarnate in an original and profound way in the depths of personal consciousness.

Donald Walhout, in a solid and useful book/87/ on Hopkins' religious experience, describes these periods of spiritual depression as "encagement," by which he means a "spiritual problem of the postcommitment religious life . . . a pervasive, spirit-depressing experience of binding confinement or overall containment." Walhout quite rightly talks of this religious experience as normal in human behavior and that for deeply religious persons with strong religious character such as Hopkins had, "encagement" generates special spiritual problems. Walhout's coinage is an apt term for Hopkins' religious mentality during the last period of his life. Throughout his religious experience up until this time Hopkins had managed to escape the mental state of "encagement" mainly through the creativity of his religious imagination, which enabled him to be transported beyond common experience to fresh spiritual intimations. Now he had fallen into the deepest "encagement" of his life. Vocation, work, friends provided very little natural enabling graces. He was left more or less to himself and his religious imagination to work his way out. And as I have suggested, his old reliance upon encounter with "mortal beauty" by his religious imagination no longer worked to satisfactory spiritual transport. He was in a deep crisis in which his very personality and his "instress-inscape" capacities seemed in deep conflict. He found himself as a Romantic personality facing what many another Romantic personality had come up against—a dulling sensibility discharging the creative imagination. Now the self becomes the theater of absurdity, and the imaginative intellect is beckoned to plunge into the phantasmagoria of the disintegrating self. Psychologically in such situations the tendency is toward self-pity and self-indulgence; artistically the inclination is toward the histrionic verbalizing of personal dementia; religiously, the direction is toward the clinging and grasping impulses of the "elective" will. All too easily self-love emerges dominant which falsely sets self–sacrifice at odds with stability, selfless creativity, and mutual love.

Such human "encagements" do require a renewed penetration of the mystery of self. This new selving means that the sense of a failed life must be faced, that the terrible pains of deeply felt desolation must be experienced. For Christians like Hopkins, if the Incarnation means Christ is in him, and it does, then for some mysterious, inexplicable reason, "immortal beauty" and "immortal diamond" had come to mean suffering to the point of spiritual death. Importantly as well, the great temptation to self-induced, personal martyrdom had to be avoided, for during such debilitating personal states release beckons as suicide, figurative or real, so easily does self-victimization dally justified surcease before the afflicted consciousness.

Desolated "encagement" is precisely what Hopkins experienced in the last years of his life. Commentators from the beginning have noted the significance of this period of Hopkins' life. (See Robinson and Walhout for the latest contrasting versions, the former secular and psychoanalytical and the latter objectively phenomenological). In encountering such deeply destructive personal and religious experience, Hopkins' religious imagination underwent alteration. Now the imagination had to "inscape" the self directly; Hopkins, the priest-poet, in a state of spiritual agony, had to be "caught," not "riding / High there" but in "his bone-house, mean-house."

This change in imaginative direction did not come easily for Hopkins. He knew all too well the experience of other Romantic personalities, especially artists, who, when they gave over their acknowledgment of objective centers to being, to reality, to self, often fell into imaginatively enhanced nightmares and effusive confessional bawling. But there was even a greater pressure on Hopkins not to concentrate on "self inscaping." For Hopkins, selfness is a form of self-affirmation, and the great danger is "self–scaping" will engender self-pride. All his poetic career Hopkins sought to counterpoise the powerful subjectivism of his Romantic personality with a strong emphasis upon objective experience, truly and objectively "seen," the real base for the generation of any validly felt transport to any transcendental spiritual intimations. Implicit in this earlier poetry is what might be called an ultrasonic aspect, a lifting-up to counter the pull of gravity of the earthly self. Hopkins' Christian Romanticism added another dimension to this imaginative equanimity, namely, a conviction that the imagination ought to be modified by the Incarnation. Just as Christ took on personhood in the natural life, giving up the prerequisites of Divinity, so the Christian poet should "empty" himself of his artistic self-pride, and merely meet his own beauty, and "Wish all, God's better beauty, grace." Hopkins felt deeply in his spiritual consciousness a powerful religious incentive to sacrifice his poetic self in imitation of Christ. I have argued in this essay, among other things, that Hopkins' formulation of a Christian Romantic synthesis was a formula of reconciliation between the intellect and the imagination, between the "elective" and "affective" wills, between the poet and the priest. Now the formula was in danger of unraveling; the two great contemplative energies of the mind could become uncycled, bringing art and philosophy at odds, and making religion and faith dichotomous. These dangers notwithstanding, the poet had to be the "dare-gale skylark," if this new religious experience was to be "instressed, stressed." The self-scape must be caught at midnight to see the swoop of "Christ-scape" in the dark.

It is within these complex contexts that Hopkins' "dark" sonnets ought to be read. They are very different religious poems from any he had written before this time. Readers and critics have noted their language differences, the leanness of their poetic forms, their concentration upon the psychological aspects of religious experience, their images of deep suffering, sorrow, and desolation. Of course, all of these attributes are noteworthy; however, I suggest that the most salient difference is that Hopkins wrote at least four of them (I place seven sonnets in the Dark Sonnet group: nos. 61, 62, 64-67, 74; see note 87) "unbidden and against my will," by which I think he meant that he could not stop his poetic "inscaping" of the desiccated religious experience he was undergoing which led him to write poetry which was personal as opposed to his earlier public poetry with its engagement with priestly ministry. He could not shut off his religious imagination which was so integral to his Romantic personality. He did not want to tell how spiritually desperate he had become, how personally desolate he felt, how hard it was for him to experience God as tester, tormentor, and judge. The other "dark poems" of this period are only slightly less "unbidden." These last poems are poems in which the Romantic religious imagination risked transport into the religious self of the poet to try to find God immanent in the darkness of anguish and desolation. The focus is upon the terrible loss of the disconnection between the "Christ-scape" and the "self-scape." This is a side to Hopkins' religious experience he never wrote about extensively until the prayerful poetic petition of Stanza 10 of "The Wreck" became personally true for him, "With an anvil-ding / And with fire in him forge they will / . . . but master him still. . . ."

The journey of the religious imagination into the spiritual self raises, as Hopkins found, grave and imponderable questions. "Carrion Comfort"/88/ is about "Christ-scape" and "self-scape." However, instead of joyous communion, the two "stresses" are "inscaped" as battling. This is most surprising, for Hopkins' religious imagination had never expressed the "Christ-scape" as a scourging, personal presence attacking the religious self, beating the spirit within an inch of its life. Heretofore, he had expressed God's mastery over natural evil. This statement of religious experience raises a major theological question about the Incarnation over which the poet puzzles. If, as Christians believe, the Incarnation means that Christ is really present in the personhood of every human being, then what is His role in such situations as Hopkins describes? Is He, the "passion plunged" Son, still undertaking his salvific ransom in the repeated mini-Passions of every human being? Or is He God the Father's envoy, delivering the message of purification by pain and suffering? The answer remains a mystery. As the poet "inscapes" this kind of religious experience, he reveals a state of physical, moral, and spiritual pressure wherein the self is punished, humiliated, and then stripped to the bare bones of his being. He tells us that in this religious state he had to fight for his very soul's existence, as if God forced him to acknowledge himself as worthwhile and lovable. He does assert his elemental integrity of being, but in remembering his ordeal he ponders why God should become a "Christ-scape" of punishment in him. Is this "God's better beauty, grace"? What is remarkable about this poem is Hopkins' depiction of God in the consciousness as a hungry, marauding beast, striking down its prey with its huge paws, pawing him again and again, all the while scanning him with wild, voracious eyes. Hopkins has here depicted a frightening religious experience, and in doing so is forced to "inscape" himself undergoing it. The religious imagination penetrates to the core of his own spiritual being with surprising results, for he dares affirm himself against what seems God's chastisements. He will not give up his being, will not become God's carrion. He would resist, would accept his self being pounded into purity: "the just man justices; / Keeps grace. . . ." And in willing his survival relief comes, as if God called it a draw, allowing him to renew his strength, and then allowing him to rejoice in his self-affirmation: "Acts in God's eye what in God's he is— / Christ."

Grace is Divine enablement freely given from the outside, but what kind of grace was this? The poet is not sure that it is only God's grace alone. For the first time in his religious experience and his imaginative expression of it, Hopkins salutes the self as hero of hard-won human "grace" able to square off and match the awesome powers of Divine grace. Hopkins' "inscaping" of his religious experience is profoundly different in these poems because his sanctifying imagination focused on self-scapes in spiritual travail. The Romantic imagination is still at work; its creative, expressional powers are directed toward the tormented "self-scape," penetrating it, elaborating it, celebrating it. The awesomeness of God's power is expressed in the poem, but so is the physical and spiritual resilience of the tortured self. Here the poet allowed himself the esthetic luxury of personal transport but without becoming solipsistic. In the "underthought" of the poem, the question of pride looms. There is a kind of Miltonic balance in the poem in which the creature squares off with the Creator and matches Him, or so it seems. It is also notable in this sonnet that the entire experience is a shocking recollection, not unlike Words-worth's sense of recollective struggle; Hopkins' recall is a journey back from absolute despair, Wordsworth's from time's weariness. This kind of religious experience, it must be emphasized again, was new to Hopkins' religious life, new to his Romantic consciousness, and new to his religious imagination. This poem, and others like it in the group, is about spiritual transport into the religious self, about the "self-scape" throttled by the immanence of Divinity.

But this "now done darkness" was not done. In the poems "No worst," "I wake and feel," and "To see the stranger"/89/ Hopkins wrote three sonnets about the suffering self as exiled and lost. They are poems in which the Romantic imagination, as foreshadowed in "Carrion Comfort," penetrates into the arid landscapes of the self and "inscapes" the hellish journey. The imagination is still religious in character, but is foreshortened in range by the sufferings of the self. God is depicted as withdrawn but His presence is powerfully felt as the mystery behind the grief, the nightmare, the insomnia, the loneliness, and the desolation. Just how very hard it is to accept personal suffering as graces to enable the devotee to rediscover God's presence, love, and care is searchingly "inscaped" in these poems of frightful religious scourging. Still Hopkins wrote them with such taut control of feeling, such leanness of language, such focused concentration, that they speak extremes through careful over- and understatement. The language of the bared self seems less poetic and more transactional.

"No worst, there is none" is a poem "inscaping" deep sorrow, one of the great poems on the subject. Though the human self has clung to its being, the price of endurance that is revealed here is very great. Grief is dramatized as a wail of witches' voices flailing the agony of being alone and afraid in the haunted self. The Romantic imagination pene-trates very deeply into the self and finds a soul-scape of heights and depths seemingly beyond human trespass. Here is the classic Romantic scene in which the hero, high upon some wild prominence, clings for his very life, not in prideful despair and surrender, but in humble self-affirmation. Hopkins, indeed, does not allow his imagination to go uncontrollably Olympian; rather, he acknowledges human finitude, gigantic as the interior human geography is, and allows the self to crawl humbly back from the precipice to hide, succor itself, and lose its pain in accepting sleep or death. Again the ghostly presence of God is felt in the poem, observing His creature enact his basic creaturehood with no hint of compassion or understanding, just as mysteriously silent as He was when Christ called out from his Cross.

In "I wake and feel" Hopkins picks up on the wretchedness of the wretch in the former poem and examines the Christ-lost self to the point of self-loathing. The religious imagination has "inscaped" the consciousness in a state of spiritual death-watch. The brooding consciousness is full of dark wakefulness which is interminable and out of which springs the spectacle of tormenting nightmare blacking out hope and indifferent to any cries of help. The consciousness is trapped in a hellish scene from which it cannot escape, a scene in which the self, separated from Christ, is depicted as nauseous, hateful, and damned. Mysteriously the marvelous salvific distinctiveness of the human personality participating in the "Christ-scape" is not felt, leaving human nature desolate, self-rejecting and death-bound. Without the Christ-yeast of God, the human spirit, as "inscaped" by Hopkins' penetrating religious imagination, is distinguished only by its own "pitch" of "selfness" whose stress is expressed as bitterness, burning, sickness. Out of this dark self-terror comes a light or grace. The religious poet construes the meaning of this night-battle as God's way of revealing the difference between acknowledging, "instressing" the "Christ-scape" in being, in the self, and not doing so. Without the Incarnation, "distressed" selfness falls into the hell of human finitude, a constant, contrary acknowledgment of limitation, failure, and loss. Creaturehood in all of its sinful fallibility is the dark light of religious nightmare in this poem, a powerful "inscape" of fallen creaturehood as a preview of everlasting hell and eternal damnation—"my taste was me." What Hopkins is distressed over is not just the disintegration of the me but "God's most deep decree": the self, elevated in God's eye, becomes in its merely human essence a very dim reflection of its original ideal because of the distancing of the individual self from God through some mysterious exile bringing disconsolation and then desolation sets in. The personality drifts away from God, its home, toward its own cave of self-centeredness. In this process the "affective" will's inclinations do not lead the person to seek God on high and His influence, but rather inclines toward the decayed, lowly state of the damned—"me-ness" without Christ.

"Carrion Comfort," "No worst," and "I wake and feel" are poems in which the religious imagination depicts the experience of deep spiritual disaffection along with the displacement of the "elective" will into serious jeopardy of its moral duty. The spiritual drama lies in the struggle to redispose the "affective" will and bring the "elective" will aright. The astringency of bitter feelings drains away the intensity of the spiritual transport beyond to Christ—God. God is "distressed" out of human experience. The religious imagination is deported to "inscape" the disenabling experience of strayed affections and the irresolutions of the free will amid the evils that the natural order sets loose. Such creative action is indeed a radical change from the soaring, enlightening spiritual dialectic of Hopkins' other sublime uses of the Christian Romantic imagination which "inscaped" so powerfully the unifying images of God in Nature and experience. Nevertheless the expression of the gloom and doom of the dark side of Nature and experience is no less genuine, religiously or esthetically. The imagination is still a sanctifying power in this poem. God, in creating everything, also made the conditions of evil, and while His deepest reasons for allowing evil to come into existence remain a mystery, still His purpose must be rooted in goodness, and therefore He must perforce use evil as a causation of His grace to give greater opportunity for union with Him. In these poems, Hopkins' religious imagination nicely sculpts the human personality in the throes of trying to seize the dark graces of deeper self-spiritualization through religious suffering in order to "instress" a greater grasping of God. He expressed a kind of spiritual surgery through which the ideal self, now cut away by self-willfulness, reunites with the "Christ-scape" tied with tighter suturing bonds. The underthought in all of these poems is the mystery of his Father dealing him "gall" and "heartburn." Was he that undeserving? Or deserving?

Some read these poems as failed religion and resurrected imagination. In this view, the priest has crashed finally because the priesthood has pushed all that was most attractive in Hopkins' personality, his poetic side, to the breaking point so that he is on the brink of spiritual and artistic suicide. Reading these poems this way in the context of Christian Romanticism, the transporting, religious imagination finally acknowledges "mortal beauty" and the human personality; instead of exclaiming the mirror image of Christ in both, the religious imagination darkens into a kind of hell of human finitude, waiting out an eternity of self-scourging. This uncharacteristic religious poetry "inscapes" melancholy, dejection, alienation, even suicide. The transporting "Christ-scape" is either a comfortless memory, proffering only absence and indifference, or a destroying leviathan, stalking its helpless prey. But in this naturalistic view the imagination has triumphed, because in these last poems Hopkins' true feeling breaks out into the open and expresses itself with great accuracy and honesty. In this reading, the dark light is secular truth revealed, the only truth. The poet triumphs.

Perhaps this is the only way the secular imagination is able to experience these poems—poems of therapy. In general these poems have received the greatest attention from those twentieth-century critics who find the experience of separation from God somehow more relevant than union with Him. Herbert Read, I. A. Richards, Daniel Harris, and J. H. Miller come to mind. Counter to such readings and attitudes, I judge these responses as mid-readings, honest, sincere, often brilliant, but nevertheless misreadings. Religious experience is at the heart of these poems. What is different is that God's presence is felt and experienced as sovereignty rather than as benevolence, omnipresence rather than immanence, judgment rather than salvation, punishment rather than comfort. The falcon of daylight has become the lion of night-light. True, the religious imagination has had to adjust from transport beyond to transport within, with the result that the "inscape" is notably changed from the earlier shapes. This alteration had to happen because the spiritual reality had changed from glorious aspiration for a "new Realism" expressed in an original individuality of expressible form to the earnest realization of God ordaining a different kind of grace (will) in which love is held in abeyance. The "deeper" form of this religious experience is self-sacrifice "inscaped" as "me frantic," "Pitched past pitch of grief," "cries countless, cries like dead letters sent / To dearest him that lives, alas! away." These poems are expressions of the completed religious experience; they show forth a dark spiritual sublimity of the graces of Christ's Passion coming to those who imitate His great sacrifice. These are Christian poems of the dark graces, as I read them.

Moreover these last sonnets retain their Romantic, Ignatian, and Scotian qualities though they are focused and applied differently than they were in the earlier poems of light. "I wake and feel" will serve as a good example of these different fusions. In the sestet the poet composes the place of his night meditation which he recollects with terrifying power, for the place "seen" by the imagination is waking up in hell. The vision is most vivid. The poet "sees" himself an outcast having fallen from the graces of his Lord. His naked soul covered in darkness, the poet cannot bear to tell of his "sights" of hell's landscape, of his frightening wanderings as he looks for some light and respite. In the second quatrain he had a more terrible "inscape" of himself as lost in hell, for the blackness of his nightmare vision discolors all his memories of all the days of his life. And what he can make out is "seen" as failure, waste, and sin. So scouring is this sense of total failure, the poet "cries" out for reprieve, for help, for forgiveness. Worse, he knows these pleas are "dead" because they are missent—they do not come out of loving contriteness but out of merciless self-loathing. Nowhere in all of his poetry did Hopkins compose a more powerful Ignatian contemplative scene, and as well, never did his Romantic consciousness show more intensely than in this poem. In these first six lines, the Romantic melancholia over unrequited love was never more plaintive to the loved one—"dearest him"—felt to be "away." What is different about these two aspects in this and nearly all the later poetry is that Hopkins shifted the place of his meditative composition from Nature to Self as did he refocus his religious imagination from Nature's "inscapes" to the "inscape of Self." Nevertheless, the same powers are at work: the imaginative consciousness penetrates directly the real experience of the "inscape of Self" to some point of deep spiritual transport into the most vivid scenes of nightmare traveling in the dark recesses of consciousness' "hell-scape."

While the imagery of the sestet is in mode medical, the application is Scotian. The first three lines present a moral analysis of those who suffer spiritual desolation. Ignatius in "Rules for the Discernment of Spirits" in his *Spiritual Exercises* noted that desolation sometimes is sent by God because of our being "tepid and slothful or negligent in our exercises," or "because God wishes to try us, to see how much we are worth," or "because God wishes to give us a true knowledge and understanding of ourselves." Whether any or all of these applied to Hopkins' spiritual life we shall never know. However we do know that in this poem he expressed in the most concrete manner the "self-scape" as being flooded with gall. With this sickening image of discoloration, nausea, and bitterness, the poet now decries the wandering, lost "self" in its Scotian "distress" of self-desolation as he had earlier celebrated the Scotian "instress" of self-consolation when he wrote of "that taste of myself, of *I* and *me* above and in all things, which is more distinctive than the taste of ale or alum, more distinctive than the smell of walnut leaf or camphor. . . . Nothing else in nature comes near this unspeakable stress of pitch, distinctiveness, and selving. . ." (*Sermons*, 123). In these last six lines of the sonnet Hopkins now depicts in stark physical imagery the nether pitch of the self left to its own self-being. Just as the Scotian sense of individuality enriched the self by his notion of univocal being shared unto God, so selving which begins to be detached through some mysterious misgiven choice or desire debilitates the self, bringing the "inscape of self" to a state of spoilage and decay. Now the physical manifestation of the self becomes "scapes" of cancerous physiology spreading corruption throughout the entire self. Scotian "me-ness" is here depicted as a spiritual leukemia.

The last three lines of the sestet closes the poem with a tormenting spiritual insight. The poet, using the image of bread (here self-made desecration), "sees" how "self-scape" is spoiled (falls rather than rises) through omitting the soul-saving yeast (grace) of the Incarnation. This is what to be damned means, what hell is about—to understand in frightening clarity the terrible fate to be abandoned to be just one's own self, as Adam and Eve felt, scripture tells us, when God decreed "sweat" to be the curse of the Fall. All at once Hopkins perceived the character of Scotian hell—"Selfyeast"—and, as well, a taste of his own desolation—"sweating selves." The meditation on Hell in its Ignatian colloquy calls for redirection to loving assent. Hopkins' poem is so burningly severe, so tormented, and painful, that unsurprisingly the colloquy is barely hinted. But it is there in the last two words of the last line, "but worse." In the depths of his hell-vision, the poet is still aware that he is not lost, not damned, not abandoned by God, for his spiritual condition, desolate as it is, is better than the damned because they are lost; he still has the promises of Christ to save him. Slight though this colloquy might seem, clearly Hopkins' revisions support this intention of drawing a clear distinction between himself and the lost souls. He felt the scourge of the lost. (Hopkins here expressed a main Ignatian point, that in spiritual desolation we can discern that most consoling affirmation of all: we really love God and cannot be happy without him.) Such a frightening sense of spiritual destiny as damnation is nearly overwhelming, but somewhere in the dark of self is Christ and His caring. Perhaps this is the darkest of the dark sonnets and, therefore, it is significant that Hopkins' religious imagination still was inspirited by his Romantic sensibility, Ignatius' meditative patterns, and Scotian "me-ness."

The other sonnets of desolation, "Patience" and "My own heart,"/90/ are remarkable for their "inscaping" the religious experience of spiritual perseverance. The religious imagination introspectively delves into the states of patience and pity as conditions of mental suffering, religious forbearance, and spiritual poise. In these sonnets, as indeed in all of the poems of this period, the poet expresses personal disconsolation to the point of destroying desolation, but disconsolation never finally dominates. The "Christ-scape" of the sun now came to Hopkins as the "Christ-scape" of the storm; how mysterious is God's mastery whether rude or merciful! The sorrows in these poems are expressed as religious wonderments and God's surcease as heavenly imponderables. The calm and acceptance so carefully "inscaped" in these poems are shown to be difficult accomplishments of the spirit and mind. The poet describes the makeup of patience as a counterpoise to external action, of which he has little. His patience is a quietly growing heart-cover which gradually hides the action inside—the war within the personality as it fights its battles on steep spiritual terrains. Hopkins depicts the "grating" and the "bruising" of self in the struggle to want God as the highest good in one's life and therefore his desire is to choose Him above all else—priesthood, poet, scholar. Yet amid all of this strife patience abides, and must, as the personality matches its patience with Divine patience, waiting for "Delicious kindness" that God "distills" for those who wait on Him, "that comes those ways we know."

"My own heart" is a poem of great religious significance among these last works of stormy graces. In it the poet enters into a kind of spiritual reconciliation with himself. He calls for self-forgiveness, kindness, charity. The grace of personal charity is the cornerstone of all religious love—the beginning of Christ-selving. The religious poet here explains the coming together of the "affective" and "elective" willpowers in the reconciling realization that playing a vengeful god to the self is a useless spiritual exercise that can become destructive. Until one perceives oneself as lovable, no comfort can be gotten or received. And lovableness does not arise from self-torment but from self-forgiveness. Here the religious poet depicts self-absolution as a step toward comfort and consolation. The religious imagination "inscapes" a wonderful sense of giving over self-pride to God's providence which moves to its own timing. The poet speaks to himself as humiliated to humbleness but lovingly with encouragements to "let joy size / At God knows when to God knows what." The religious imagination captures the intimation of grace proffered in some unexpected future moment bringing to the "Soul, self" a glimpse of some beatific landscape. This poem in this group of poems is important, for it marks a new spiritual stability earned at great personal price. The worst was over; the poet felt the "I/Me" moving towards a new unifying self, free at last in the freedom of loving surrender—me-ness to Christ-ness.

These two poems are expressions of spiritual renewal, poems in which the religious poet "inscapes" the personality undergoing a reconstruction after a terrible purging. The self has been reamed out almost to the point of self-destruction but now, in its more pure state, the personality is more open to relocate in itself and its experience the "Christ-scape" ever shining from behind the stormy ramparts of personal existence. What a triumph for the Christian religious imagination! The great danger was that in the redirection from the ascending imagination catching the "Christ-scapes" in the outer world, that wondrous swim to within sight of some eternal visionary shore, the descending imagination would plunge into some inner wallow, that dark sink drained of the waters of love and forgiveness, where the distraught poet would beat his heart in spite of God, the world, even himself. These poems are not just cries from a flogged man feeling torment, damnation, and creative crisis. There are these elements in this group of poems, but in all of them there is the search for passage beyond a state of guilt and ruin to a state of renewal of the poet's "goings" in grace, for some glimpse of Christ housed in his life and experiences in his alien circumstances, for the warming "smile" of charity. The poet and priest, who had earlier announced with the strongest confidence the Incarnation surfacing in everything and everybody, now is able to speak with newly and dearly earned spiritual calm and forbearance that his self is open to a deeper spiritual tenderness and greater sacrificial love of God. There is even in this self-sacrifice a kind of self-affirmation arising out of a newly achieved self-control in which the poet depicts himself trying to "out-patient" God, or at least having become so docile and patient and kind that God cannot refrain from "lighting a lovely mile." These poems of stormy religious grace are authentic instances of the creativity of Hopkins' Christian Romantic imagination because they are grounded in the realism of true religious experiences in which his imagination engages earnestly and probes deeply for the Christocentric spiritual patterns of sanctification, and finally "inscapes" them honestly, sincerely, and accurately in original esthetic forms of great individuality.

With these poems Hopkins' Christian Romantic imagination came full circle—the religious experience of the "Christ-scape" of Christmas to the "Christ-scape" of Easter. Hopkins' religious experience moved beyond the happy days of Christ playing "in ten thousand places," and therefore his religious imagination produced no longer the "inscapes" of the soaring, shining glow of the Incarnation basking in the lights of the world. These last poems are Good Friday poems, religious expressions of the soul and body bruised and battered in a personal version of the Incarnation crucified.

The personal crisis this religious experience affords is that of a devastating new awareness of the dangerous finitude of the human predicament and the absolute dependence of the human self on the saving graces of Christ's liberation. Hopkins' religious imagination "inscaped" this state of human helplessness in "That Nature is a Heraclitean Fire and of the Comfort of the Resurrection."/91/ In this sonnet written while deep in his depression (July 1888), Hopkins again "sees" into Nature and discovers anew the grand cosmic festival of air, water, fire, and earth. Once more he is awed with the power and majesty of the spectacle of "mortal" beauty. But this time there is no ascending transport to Christ playing in ten thousand places; rather there is the frightening sense of the deep fire of natural being alternately building and burning out of sight and out of mind. Mortal Nature in all her Mortal Beauty is a mysterious phoenix dying and rising in the fire of her being, God's tiger burning bright. Not so "Manshape." The mortal beauty of humanity is end-stopped in dark oblivion. Trapped with seeing the Christological "inscapes" deep down Nature, Hopkins' religious experience does not engender a spiritual transport through Nature to a transcendental awareness of the Christ-image in all things. Christ no longer is seen as the main actor in the theater of Nature. But still he believes in Christ Incarnate, still he must rely on Him to snatch his heart and soul out of the furnace of natural Creation. Suddenly there is a felt source of connection, of communication, of enablement, which engulfs his feeling of personal hopelessness and spiritual foundering. Christ is hidden in the deep structure of Nature, is the "stress" of his being and all being, flashes through corresponding grace (a gift outright of God's saving love). His eastering self as the very image and likeness of the foundering soul that "nature's bonfire" is purifying to realize its true and real identity— "Christ *being me* and me being Christ." In no poem is spiritual transport more sudden, dramatic, and transfiguring than in the last lines where the poet affirms the Incarnation and its intense, sanctifying effect upon the religious consciousness. Hopkins' alchemical typology brilliantly translates the religious meaning of the Incarnation transforming the Christian Romantic consciousness with utterance of the Word.

This spiritual affirmation of the Christian religious consciousness may seem much like the others we have seen in the earlier poems, the same movement from the Ignatian spiritualizing composition of place to some transcendent intimation of Christ. However, I suggest the spiritual transport in this poem is different. The poet feels as never before end-stopped in his reaching and grasping for the "Christ-scape" in Nature. There seems to be no religio-imaginative enablement of grace to energize spiritual transport. The poet's religio-sense experience is discontinuous; he has to wait for help, affirmation, rescue, from the outside. There seems to be, in this poem and others of this period, more of a reliance upon an abstract assurance through faith in some transcendental powers coming to the rescue. The powerful heightening at the end of the poem is deeply felt, sincere, but the reader feels that the individual resurrection emerges out of the religious mystery of the Resurrection more on the basis of faith (the "elective" will) than out of belief arising from direct religious experience (the "affective" will). This is a different use of the religious imagination in which the poet is reaching out because his reaching within is becoming spiritually sterile and unproductive. In this poem Hopkins expressed a felt and found consolation, but there is a "last reprieve" desperateness in its tone. Now, like the tall nun on the *Deutschland,* he was off that "pastoral forehead in Wales"; he was foundering on the storm-wracked deck of his own life. The religious experience was new and different; it forced upon him changes in his uses of the religious imagination to "inscape" spiritual extremity as he experienced it.

However, there are other poems in this last group which are intimations of consolation beyond this desolated religious state. "St. Alphonsus Rodriguez"/92/ is a poem about religious perseverance. Hopkins, through his saintly intercessor St. Alphonsus, acknowledges that in God's providence he was not to produce great scholarship or perform significant priestly acts; more especially, he was not to awaken bone-bound mankind on the battlefield of life to the exploits of Christ. Yet he, like Alphonsus, fought a battle no less ferocious, "the war within" that is hidden, silent, requiring the heroic breast to be inwardly-steeled to achieve that victory of self-conquest, total submission to the will of God, even if it required the devastation of all honor "flashed off exploit." Hopkins asserts in this poem the great spiritual victory of absolute self-sacrifice in God's name that Alphonsus achieved. The religious integrity of such devotion as expressed in the poem reveals a deep awareness of Hopkins' increasing appreciation and understanding of his own religious service, his own dedication, and the great reward of spiritual perseverance.

The last three poems in Hopkins' mature canon/93/ together with "St. Alphonsus," are Holy Saturday poems, that is, they are "inscapes" of the religious experience of spiritual numbness, prayerful watching, wondrous hopes, Jobian questionings, and prayerful petitions for purification. "Thou art indeed just" is a sign that Hopkins had regained his spiritual composure. Taking off from the Biblical epigraph, Hopkins states with great pertinency the argument for moral justice to be rendered to the just of this world. But in making the case, Hopkins really states the anomaly of Divine justice and the mystery of Divine love. This poem is a Holy Saturday poem because it is really about grace, that Deific deliverance from the time–strain of Nature's cycle. The poet's call from his entombed self for the waters of grace is a powerful sign of his movement toward a resurrected liberation. He knows it is God's gift to give.

"The shepherd's brow" is an important poem in this group and is rightly restored to its proper place. In it, Hopkins restates what to him are the "facts" of creature-hood: God created, mankind fell, nature is no paradise, and human nature is not angelic. In sum, the human condition is tragic. This hard look at the worst of the human predica-ment is the very ground of all religion, the very source of what Donald Walhout calls "encagement." Without the recognition of the limits of human life, without an objective perception of the sacral essence of human nature, creature-hood is unacknowledged and human life is reduced to absurdity and despair, death its mockery. Religious motiva-tion arises from this realism because the recognition of human finitude in all of its natural detail and incident causes the heart and soul to cast for comfort beyond self and the natural world. In this poem Hopkins "inscaped" mankind in the world, fallen and smeared, a stark reminder of his own humanness, a jarring insight to naturality apart from God. This is a Holy Saturday spiritual reflection, the kind of meditation which intensifies the meaning of Good Friday, the day of the death of the Savior, and Easter Sunday, the day of "immortal diamond."

Many modern readers see no Easter Sunday in Hopkins' religious poetry. They read what became his farewell, "To R. B.," as a statement of personal, religious, and poetic emasculation. Many contemporary secular critics praise these last poems of dread more highly than the earlier poems of Christian love. They also decry the personal circumstances out of which they were produced. Much of this critical approval arises from a rejection, or the serious doubting, of the Christian Romanticism which is at the core of Hopkins' religious imagination.

"To R. B." in my reading is a poem about his creative imagination. The first quatrain is Hopkins' poetic version of

Coleridge's Primary and Secondary Imagination. Hopkins used the figuration of sexual imagery, "blowpipe flame," to make translucent the penetrative potency of the Primary Imagination as he used "the mind a mother" as the figure for the Secondary Imagination gestating the newly conceived word. Hopkins here revealed his own experience of poetic energy as a sudden and special "instress" or penetrative perception through which he obtained an original insight into the inmost nature of some distinctive feature of some datum within his experience. The figure suggests intensity, torrid heat, and intense light. Applying the figuration to the creative act, he suggests unbidden awarenesses blasting his consciousness and generating in him powerful feelings simultaneous with flashes of rare intelligibility, all of these accumulating and fusing into a kind of densely packed illuminative consciousness. Coleridge described this creative state as "a repetition in the finite mind of the eternal act of creation in the infinite I AM." Existence is seen as a matrix in which individual things are perceived as they exactly are and yet, viewed vertically, they become transfigured up through the cognitive matrix by the symbolizing imagination into a "living form" keying all Creation. As we have seen, to Hopkins this arch-center of Being is the Incarnation. This last sonnet makes clear that for Hopkins poetic energy meant a powerful burst of perception producing the inspired kind of poetic art he sought to make—a "live and lancing" perceptiveness sustained to the level of a unified experience, "the incomprehensible Certainty," whose symbolization is the Word within the word.

Once this "Spur" or engendering perception of the Primary Imagination occurs, the poet tells us, the mothering Secondary Imagination unerringly bears the mysterious conception to its birthing utterance. Hopkins makes, in his figure of the Secondary Imagination, a widow of this faculty, suggesting that the archetypical pattern of his sexual imagery is the Christian mystery of the Annunciation rather than the unmysterious pattern of natural sexuality. The widowhood Hopkins describes suggests something of the reverence and humility which characterized a holy or blessed state of creative consciousness, an inseminating spiritual inspiration gradually being made flesh (word) as the mothering mind "wears, bears, cares and combs. . . ."

Hopkins' last poem, of course, is a lament over the absence of this "blowpipe flame" of the creative imagination. He probably felt the diminishment of his creative powers more keenly when he wrote the sonnet, for he was already ill with the typhoid fever that was to kill him about six weeks later. Are we to read this last poem as Hopkins' final statement about all the poetry he wrote in Ireland? I think not. Indeed the poem is about loss of poetic power, but it is also an impressive exercise of poetic power. He knew that his poem was telling of a major shift in his religious experience which had produced a significant alteration in the use of his religious imagination, a movement from "instressing" Christ in the self to "instressing" the self in Christ. The former religio-imaginative experience is one of joyful recognition of the Incarnation and the latter is one of sorrowful recognition of the mystery of Christ's Passion, both segments of the full Christian experience. Still, Hopkins quite understandably longed for that "fine delight" of the windhover Christ rather than that of "winter world" of the Dublin Christ. Both kinds of religious experience were the bases of powerful religious poetry that possesses the highest artistic powers. Indeed, Hopkins became in the combination of his celebratory and suffering poetic sides the complete Christian Romantic poet, for he both experienced profoundly and expressed finely the two classic states of Christian spirituality—the suffering Desolation of Good Friday and the glorious consolation of Easter Sunday: "O pity and indignation!" and "In a flash, at a trumpet crash, / I am all at once what Christ is . . . immortal diamond."

Hopkins was a unique Victorian. His was an original Christian Romantic consciousness out of which he produced a remarkable body of writing—letters, journals, notes, commentaries, criticism, and poetry. Together they add up to an imposing body of letters establishing Hopkins as a Victorian poet of the first rank. He has added stature in that modern readers have found his poetry surprisingly current. His modern relevance is not just the result of the accidents of his publishing history. The essential reason is the modernity of his creative intellect. While it is true early critics found his poetic style particularly suitable to the theory of poetry they were espousing—poetry with rich surface patterns and dense linguistic structures—as his writings became fully known and understood, more and more readers found in his work, indeed in his life, what can only be called real experience, truly encountered and strongly penetrated, the very stuff which is the living form of the human consciousness caught in new light and fresh expression, plumbed at new heights and depths. This "new Realism," as he called it, is at the heart of the modern matter.

XIII

I have tried to show in this essay that Hopkins was a high English Romantic. He possessed that quality of imagination in the tradition of Blake, Wordsworth, and Coleridge, namely, the power to express in original poetic forms the movements of the religious consciousness through states of spiritual transport that emanated out of emotional and visual experience possessing a sacral character. But I have argued as well that Hopkins is a unique Romantic. First of all, he was consummately Christian in outlook, and second, he sought to synthesize the Romantic spirit within the main philosophic direction of Western culture, rationalism. He saw clearly the need to authenticate Romantic consciousness by grounding it in the real experience of objective reality. He called for a Christian "new Realism" in order to bring together the two modes of human intellectual energy—ideas and facts—into some meaningful union which would fully integrate personality and culture. Though he never completed a formal statement of his thinking, Hopkins did attempt to base all of his writing and work on an original philosophical synthesis. Thus in his uses of the creative imagination he stressed perception as objectively real and individuality that has a metaphysical essence. The imagination, Hopkins believed, delves into these realities and re-expresses them in new "inscapes." Unlike many Romantics, awash in philosophical confusion, Hopkins disallowed any sense that the imagination was a way to indulge fancy.

This unique fusion of sound rationalism and Christian Romanticism (a creative fusion of pure reason and the visionary imagination), because it arises from an authentic engagement with real experience, makes Hopkins' art very imposing. So often, even in great literary artists, thinking is murky and unclear so that the range of responses to their art makes it dificult to place their imaginative acts in convincing contexts of real experience. We are left to play at a distance their imaginative world against the real world of experience in order to discover any comprehensive view of reality. Frequently we cannot find any steady perspective about what such an author considers truly real with the result that his art often diminishes to fancy, reverie, or consciousness flow, what Ruskin called the "Pathetic fallacy."

Despite the fact that Hopkins never completed in a finished form of expression a synthesis of his world-view, he most definitely possessed such a perspective. His was not just a philosophy in a technical sense, but rather he had worked out a total philosophy of life/94/ which, to be truly valid, must comprehend an origin to existence, an understanding of the state of natural and human life, and an ultimate end to which all existence is directed. A philosophy of life, thus, is compounded of a rational view of real existence including the human components plus a vision which gives full and fulfilling meaning to the finitude discoverable in all awareness of natural and human existence. This is another way of saying that human reason and will must be cooperatively conjoined in order to see the world steady and whole.

However, Hopkins would not stop with the limits of reason. In its own proper sphere the reason understands objective reality but runs into problems which are ultimately insoluble through reason alone. Causality must give way to higher probabilities. Higher meaning and purpose emerge only if religious truth is brought to bear upon the imponderables of human reasoning. The result of such an amalgamation is an erection of a single and unified understanding of the world. God created the world, humans marred the world, and Christ came to share with humanity the mending of it. Once assent is made to this major insight, then an order of living emerges. The central and ultimate purpose of all existence is to relate to God with full devotion and service. Everything, thought, word, and deed must enter into this relationship. Such was Hopkins' philosophy of life.

In directing all life to realize Divinity, there are teachings, practices, and personal habits which are enablements or facilitators in promoting the praise and service of God. For Hopkins this meant the Bible, the Christian tradition of spirituality and community, and Ignatian meditation. From this state of intellective will, Hopkins developed answers to questions posed by his intellective reason. He explained why things are distinctive, how they are scaled in existence, how God really participates in the real being of existence, how we can discern the Divine in the real, how we can and should respond to what we sense. He had a view about the nature of God, how God relates to creation, what is meant by His providence, and why God is as well the author of evil as good. Hopkins especially had developed a view of God's most powerful participation in His Creation, namely Jesus, who is a direct reflection of God and a model for all creation, especially mankind. Christ, therefore, is our leader, and to follow Him means to purify natural desire and choice to reach His purity of reflection of God. The constant in this spiritual path is sacrifice. In accomplishing this ultimately sublime endeavor for human elevation, one must constantly raise the powers of selfhood, which means coping with the real powers of freedom in the personality so that loving and serving God is ever the shaping ideal in our journey into self-realization, that the consciousness is ever ready and willing to respond to whatever aid, enablement, encouragement, or grace God might proffer.

Briefly, these tenets were Hopkins' world-view. He held them seriously and earnestly, which is to say that he held them to be truth. Moreover, they constantly and powerfully informed all his writing, particularly his poetry. He knew, therefore, that this poetry was different from much of what was being written in his time because he felt

110

certain about that which many other writers felt uncertain of. This is why there emerged gradually in his mind and world a need for what he called a "new Realism." Though he himself was disappointed with the degree of scholarly and artistic realization of his world-view, I have been arguing that he did in fact realize a powerful statement of his thinking in his poetry if read in the context of his letters and papers. Almost from the beginning of his mature intellectual and artistic consciousness, I submit that he began to develop an original Christian, modern consciousness affirming that there is an authentication in real experience of a divine dimension reflected in Nature and selfhood, discoverable through the powerful effect of a kind of transport to a visionary experience beyond experience—from natural sense to supernatural sense, from an immanent to a transcendental affirmation of Divinity participating in the real world. I have called this conjunction of understandings through reason and transports through the imagination a Christian Romantic consciousness.

Much of this analysis contends with secular responses to Hopkins' writings in general and his poetry in particular, especially his last poems. So much critical response to the last segment of Hopkins' mature poetry is positive and receptive for the wrong reasons. I argue that the last poems are no less powerful affirmations of his "new Realism" than the earlier ones. In fact, I believe they authenticate and validate Hopkins' religious imagination in ways not achieved before. They state powerfully the religious phenomenology of the total Christian spiritual life as Hopkins experienced it. He depicted in the last poems through his religious imagination the pattern and character of interior life involved in the human personality when there is spiritual division, anxiety, depression, and disconsolation. Just as the earlier poems celebrate the brilliant charge of God's grandeur in everything, however indifferent the human consciousness is to that Divine participation, so in these last poems Hopkins dramatizes the felt experience of the dark charge of God's grandeur, however difficult in the human consciousness is this Divine participation. The seeing and seizing these moments through the "inscaping" of the religious imagination, I assert, is as well a creative realization of the higher Romantic imagination. So much Romantic poetry is not this powerful fusion of personality and real experience; rather so much of such poetry is the rumbling and wailing of the human personality at a lower human plane that much of it can be dismissed as an esthetic version of psychic disturbance. This kind of solipsistic use of the creative imagination has challenged the validity of the Romantic heritage, especially in the eyes of the scientific rationalists. The result is a critical muddle in which modern readers, while aspiring to keep intact the esthetic traditions of the Romantic imagination, are at the same time implicit assenters to forms of rationalism which either contradict the spiritual idealism in Romanticism or reduce Romanticism to expressions of esthetic therapy. True feelings are celebrated but no truth is vested in them.

It is in this latter guise that so many contemporary readers praise Hopkins' last poems by making them submit to that version of decayed Romanticism which still pervades to the minds of those permeated with some contemporary positivism. To such readers these last poems possess psychological attributes of personal decompensation expressed in compelling, astringent verbal forms readily reducible to some stereotypes of modern psychoanalysis. The earlier poems of visionary religious transcendence do not so comply and thus seem less remarkable. To such modern minds, schooled in scientism, these earlier exuberant, religious poems of transport, dramatizing the direct encounter of an awful power in but beyond experience, cannot be schematized or diagrammed. Admittedly the character of such extraordinary experience transforms the expressive, creative powers of imagination so that the art produced is uncontrollable by ordinary linguistic formulas. However, verbal accessibility is really not the main issue here. What is is the presupposition that since transcendent awareness cannot be authenticated in ordinary sight and sense, and since it seems impossible to validate scientifically the visionary awareness in such poetry, it is no more than bravura.

Either unaware of or following this contradictory view of Romanticism, many modern readers and critics praise

Hopkins for his last poems which seem to state a breakdown of his Romantic realism. They enthuse over his powerful expressions of tension and suffering; they find these poems of "wrecked past purpose" somehow triumphant, even though the triumph is based upon, in this view, failure of the most destructive kind, that of his priestly and poetic vocations. How ironical all this praise is for poems which are so replete with such monumental spiritual meaning, poems in which the religious imagination is so powerfully expressive of the dark side of the religious life, poems which indeed possess their own special spiritual beauties. These poems are, of course, ever so penetrating expressions of the soul's torments, and I do not quarrel with those readers who see this clearly, but I do quarrel with those who praise them primarily as the poet's finally having come around to coping with the reality of human absurdity. Such readers miss the Easter Sunday in them, the "morning, at the brown brink eastward . . . ," the sanctifying imagination.

Hopkins' poetry is not merely dreaming, nor is it just high minded flux. His poetry is a complex drama in which a simple and common moment is shown to be, in being what it is, a hallowing perceptive moment in which the poet's consciousness captures thing, thought, feeling, and symbol in one cross-sectioned grasp of awesome, imaginative intellection. His poems are dramatizations of a religious mode of the imagination penetrating into human experience with the richest simultaneous apprehensions which, taken together, form a vision, the very touchstone of those poets we rightly call prophetic visionaries. For these unusual poets truly "stare" into the Light of the Universe. Moreover, their poetic visions produce enormous hope in the human breast. In them our common humanity is confirmed and our Divine destiny promised. In short, we are redeemed through the marvelous powers of the creative religious imagination penetrating the experiencing self to an enlightened moment of sanctifying self-discovery.

At the outset of this long analysis, I suggested that Hopkins is a member of that group of poets Harold Bloom has called "the visionary company." In this essay I have tried to show how Hopkins' religious imagination created a vision of Christ in all of His visible dimensions while simultaneously revealing Him as one and whole with the invisible Father before all ages. I reiterate my assertion about Hopkins' membership in Bloom's special company, for Hopkins' poetry possesses the credentials Bloom lays down for membership: "a vision, a way of seeing, and of living, a more human life." Which of the Romantic poets, whether in the high or low mode, ever put human life in such a privileged place as did Hopkins when he summed up all the visions of all "the visionary company" by saying, "I am all at once what Christ is, since he was what I am . . . immortal diamond"? This is the holy vision which is expressed in the complex drama of Hopkins' poetry.

In Hopkins' poetic art the humanization of Christ that is in Blake, the religious uses of Nature that are in Wordsworth, the symbolic and illative imaginative intellects that are in Coleridge and Newman, all reach their fullest realizations. Bloom notwithstanding, Hopkins is the Victorian bridge to the visionary poets of the twentieth century, for he has through his poetry made translucent what he called "the incomprehensible Certainty" of Christ "buckling" self and soul, Nature and Super-Nature, Time and Eternity, into one Supreme Truth—the final good in human existence itself, the Incarnation. Those poets (and critics as well) who have come after him in this century for the most part can only gaze and wonder over the rich inlays of his sanctifying poems while dreaming longingly out of themselves a hope that their supreme fictions might "find [such] a good in human existence itself."/95/ However, many of us, like Robert Bridges, still stare blankly at Hopkins' "heavenward flight."

XIV

Gerald Manley Hopkins is a poet for our time. His poetry is very cogent for modern readers because we still live in the legacy of Romanticism. Despite the heavy overlay of science and materialism on contemporary culture, there still lives "deep down" a strong personal sense of unseen powers in Nature which can transform human consciousness; a hope still thrives that there is rescue from

114

heartless scientism and headless humanism. In general this reaching down and out is in keeping with the Romantic spirit which in its purest vein is an aspiration to discover and celebrate through the senses a path of personal transport from the beauty of natural experience to the sublimity of supernatural awareness. This is precisely why Hopkins and his poetry are so modern. The unique, dramatic thrust of Hopkins' art is his attempt to validate the Christian claim to the reality of an Incarnated God, a Divinity who enters into the natural and human states. If such an awesome event has taken place, then all human experience has been transformed and human consciousness has been transfigured. The Romantic "visionary gleam" is truly the Light of the World.

For over two hundred years now, the Romantic tradition of spirit and mind and letters has called for something more meaningful to the world than science and materialism, something more purposeful to human life than old age and death, something more lastingly beautiful than natural beauty. Hopkins' poetry is an imposing modern witness to this possibility; through his religious imagination he speaks with great and beautiful affirmation of the single and ultimate end of human destiny as "immortal beauty" and "immortal diamond": "Somewhere else there is ah well where! one, / One. Yes, I can tell such a key, I do know such a place...."/96/ This is the great challenge of Hopkins' art—will we "rear wings bolder and bolder" or will we black out in "Unchrist, all rolled in ruin"? He saw plainly and stated incisively the prize which the human soul (Christian and non-Christian) has been seeking—and still seeks. No wonder that Hopkins is looked upon as the major religious poet of this and the last century.

NOTES

Gratitude is here expressed to the Society of Jesus for the "fair use" of quotations from G. M. Hopkins' poetry and prose, and to all authors and publishers whose work I have quoted and cited, and to Diane M. Azevedo and Shirley Mills for excellent assistance in preparing the text.

/1/Among numerous valuable books, I have made most use of Stephen Prickett's *Romanticism and Religion: The Tradition of Coleridge and Wordsworth in the Victorian Church* (N.Y.: Cambridge University Press, 1976); also his *Coleridge and Wordsworth. The Poetry of Growth* (Cambridge: Cambridge University Press, 1970). Also Basil Willey, *Samuel Taylor Coleridge* (N.Y.: Norton 1972); Owen Barfield, *What Coleridge Thought* (Oxford University Press, 1972); Thomas McFarland, *Coleridge and the Pantheist Tradition* (Oxford: Clarendon Press, 1969); John Coulson, *Newman and the Common Tradition* (Oxford: Clarendon Press, 1970); David Ferry, *The Limits of Mortality* (Middletown, Conn.: Wesleyan University Press, 1959); Geoffrey Hartman, *Wordsworth's Poetry, 1787-1814* (New Haven: Yale University Press, 1964). Other sources used are Harold Bloom, *The Visionary Company: A Reading of English Romantic Poetry* (revised and enlarged; Ithaca: Cornell University Press, 1972); M. H. Abrams, *Natural Supernaturalism: Tradition and Revolution in Romantic Literature* (N.Y.: W. W. Norton, 1971); F. X. Shea, S. J., "Religion and the Romantic Movement," *Studies in Romanticism* IX (Fall 1970) 185-97. This issue on Romanticism is generally useful, especially Shea's article from which I have borrowed liberally.

There is ample evidence that Hopkins had read Wordsworth and Coleridge in some depth. In 1865 he wrote an undergraduate essay on poetic diction based principally on Wordsworth; he also makes references to Coleridge (see Hopkins' *Papers,* pp. 84-5, as cited in note 21). Hopkins also refers to Coleridge in his *Letters to Bridges* (p. 250, as cited in not 32); he wrote to R. W. Dixon about Coleridge's notions of prosody and his principles of criticism (*Letters to Dixon,* pp. 18, 173, 121, as cited in note 2). In a long letter to Coventry Patmore on May 6, 1888, Hopkins discussed in considerable detail the English Romantics; his main focus was on Keats (whose "verse is at every turn abandoning itself to an unmanly and enervating luxury" *(Further Letters,* pp. 385-87, as cited in note 33). Hopkins makes reference to Wordsworth in his letters to Bridges and Dixon 25 times, 8 times in his miscellaneous letters, 15 in his papers; he references Coleridge 8 times to Bridges and Dixon, 4 in his miscellaneous letters, and once in his papers. The citations suggest that Hopkins had a working familiarity with the writings of these great English Romantics.

/2/*The Correspondance of G. M. Hopkins and R. W. Dixon,* ed. C. C. Abbott (London: Oxford University Press, 1955), pp. 147-48. Hereafter *Dixon.*

/3/Prickett, *Romanticism,* p. 87.

/4/*Dixon,* op. cit.

/5/Prickett, *Romanticism,* p. 18.

/6/Ibid.

/7/Prickett, *Romanticism,* p. 19.

/8/Prickett, *Romanticism,* p. 28.

/9/See Wilfrid Ward, *The Life of John Henry Cardinal Newman* (Longmans, Green & Co., 1912), II, pp. 336 ff.; Prickett also discusses Newman's childhood in relation to Wordsworth, *Romanticism,* pp. 175-76.

/10/Prickett, *Romanticism,* pp. 190-91. Newman's psychology of religion is expertly discussed by M. J. Svaglic in his edition of Newman's *Apologia Pro Vita Sua* (London: Oxford University Press, 1967) and in C. F. Harrold's edition of a *A Grammar of Assent* (London: Longman, 1957).

/11/Prickett, *Romanticism,* pp. 194-95.

/12/Ibid.

/13/Prickett, *Romanticism*, p. 208.

/14/Prickett, *Romanticism*, p. 13.

/15/Bloom, pp. xx–xxv.

/16/*Poems of Gerard Manley Hopkins*, edited with addi-
tional notes, a forward on the revised text, and a new biographical and critical introduction, by W. H. Gardner and N.
H. MacKenzie (4th ed.; London: Oxford University Press,
1967), p. 5. Hereafter, *Poems*.

/17/Elisabeth W. Schneider, *The Dragon in the Gate:
Studies in the Poetry of G. M. Hopkins* (Perspectives in
Criticism 20; Berkeley: University of California Press,
1968), p. 5; John Robinson, *In Extremity: A Study of Gerard
Manley Hopkins* (Cambridge: Cambridge University Press,
1978), pp. 7–8.

/18/*Poems*, p. 3.

/19/*Poems*, p. 26.

/20/*Poems*, p. 31.

/21/*The Journals and Papers of Gerard Manley Hopkins*,
ed. Humphrey House, completed by Graham Storey (2d. ed.,
revised and enlarged; London: Oxford University Press,
1959), pp. 4–16, for example. Hereafter, *Papers*. See also
James Milroy, *The Language of Gerard Manley Hopkins* in
The Language Library, ed. Eric Partridge (London: Andre
Deutsch, 1970) for an extended discussion of the general
development of Hopkins' language, and his "Hopkins' Victorian Language," in *The Hopkins Quarterly* I, no. 4 (1975)
167–82.

/22/*Papers*, pp. 115–17.

/23/*Papers*, p. 116.

/24/Ibid.

/25/*Papers*, p. 117.

/26/*Papers*, pp. 118–21.

/27/See Geoffrey H. Hartman, "Introduction: Poetry and Justification," in *Hopkins: A Collection of Critical Essays*, ed. Geoffrey H. Hartman (Englewood Cliffs, N.J.: Prentice-Hall, 1966) pp. 1–15. Also Louise Rader, "Romantic Structure and Theme in Hopkins' Poetry," *The Hopkins Quarterly* I, no. 2 (1974) 93–109.

/28/*Papers*, pp. 128–30.

/29/*Papers*, p. 129. Coleridge, in his "Theory of Life," states that the "law of life" is a relationship of tension between "individuation" and "the power which unites a given *all* into a whole that is presupposed by all its parts." This notion is very close to Hopkins' idea of "inscape" and "instress," the "thisness" of the individual in tension between opposite powers. See Prickett, *Romanticism*, p. 23.

/30/Hopkins' direct statements about the Imagination were made in the context of other subjects. In a lengthy note on contemplating the Nativity of Christ in the Second Week of the *Spiritual Exercises*, he followed Scotus in discussing the three faculties of the mind: the memory, the understanding, and the will. The Imagination he makes a particular power of the Memory: "towards things future or things unknown or imaginary is Imagination. When continued or kept on the strain the act of this faculty is attention, adventure, heed, the being *ware* and its habit, knowledge, the being *aware*. Towards God it gives rise to reverence, it is the sense of *presence* of God." See *The Sermons and Devotional Writings of Gerard Manley Hopkins*, ed. Christopher Devlin (London: Oxford University Press, 1959), pp. 124, 298. Hereafter, *Sermons*.

In another place on commenting on the *Spiritual Exercises*, "The Discernment of Spirits," Hopkins remarks on Rule 1, which touches on the use of the imagination in provoking sin through "sensual gratification": " 'Imagination' —Here St. Ingatius does speak of the lower, not the intellectual, imagination. . . ." Fr. Devlin comments, "GMH's theory of the affective will, and indeed his whole outlook as a poet made it necessary for him to hold that the imagination expresses the language of the spirit as well as those of the body. Here, as elsewhere, he is anxious to enlist St. Ignatius on his side" (*Sermons*, pp. 203, 205, 310). These notes as well as his other applied understandings of the nature, role, and power of the Imagination are basically compatible with Wordsworth, Coleridge, and Newman. However, though Hopkins' approach is specifically Scotistic and Ignatian, his notion of the Imagination and the real exercise of its powers demonstrates what Coleridge meant by the essentially religious character of the Imagination, its intellective aspects, and its symbolizing powers to make translucent the "Special in the Individual, or of the General in the Especial, or of the Universal in the General."

/31/See the discussions of Hopkins and Scotus by Christopher Devlin in *Sermons*, pp. 338-52, as well as comments made in the introductions to each part. Devlin has also done major scholarship on Scotus and Hopkins. See David A. Downes, *Gerard Manley Hopkins: A Study of His Ignatian Spirit* (N.Y.: Bookman Associates-Twayne, 1960), pp. 188-89. See also my *Victorian Portraits: Hopkins and Pater* (N.Y.: Bookman Associates-Twayne, 1965), pp. 70-73, 93-100.

/32/*The Letters of Gerard Manley Hopkins to Robert Bridges*, ed. C. C. Abbott (2d ed.; London: Oxford University Press, 1955), p. 5. Hereafter, *Bridges*.

/33/*Further Letters of Gerard Manley Hopkins*, ed. C. C. Abbott (enlarged 2d edition; London: Oxford University Press, 1956), p. 58. Hereafter, *Further Letters*.

/34/*Further Letters*, p. 412.

/35/*Sermons*, pp. 209, 312.

/36/See Downes, *Ignatian Spirit*, chapter 2.

/37/*Papers*, pp. 125-26.

/38/*Papers*, p. 126.

/39/Ibid.

/40/*Papers*, p. 129

/41/Robinson, pp. 22-24.

/42/Downes, *Ignatian Spirit*, pp. 73-80; also chapter 6.

/43/See a more recent restatement in my essay, "Beatific Landscapes in Hopkins," *The Hopkins Quarterly* I, nos. 3 and 4 (1974-75) 137-60; 185-201.

/44/*Papers*, p. 120. See *Sermons*, pp. xiii, 292 for information on Hopkins and his scholastic preceptors.

/45/*Papers*, pp. 221, 236, 249. Also see *Sermons* appendix II for an expert analysis of Scotus and Hopkins.

/46/*Papers*, p. 125.

/47/*Papers*, p. 126.

/48/Ibid.

/49/*Papers*, p. 126.

/50/Robinson, pp. 24-33.

/51/See Downes, *Victorian Portraits*, pp. 117-27.

/52/Robinson, p. 30.

/53/David A. Downes, *The Temper of Victorian Belief: Studies in the Religious Novels of Pater, Kingsley, and Newman* (N.Y.: Twayne, 1972).

/54/The most extensive discussion of "Incarnationalism" in Hopkins scholarship is James Finn Cotter, *Inscape: The Christology and Poetry of Gerard Manley Hopkins* (Pittsburg: University of Pittsburg Press, 1972), sections entitled "Christology," pp. 3-143.

/55/See Cotter's helpful discussion of St. John and "The Wreck," chapters 4 and 7.

/56/Robinson, pp. 116-19; Schneider, pp. 26-33.

/57/Robinson, pp. 118-19.

/58/Robinson, p. 121.

/59/*Poems*, pp. 64, 78, 89, 90.

/60/*Poems*, p. 66.

/61/*Poems*, pp. 66, 67, 70, 71, 90, 91.

/62/*Poems*, p. 69.

/63/See Devlin, 115-21; Robinson, chapter 5; Bernard Bergonzi, *Gerard Manley Hopkins* (in Masters of World Literature Series, ed. Louis Kronenburger; N.Y.: Collier Books, 1977), chapter 5.

/64/*Poems*, pp. 76, 72. Michael Moore has suggested that Hopkins' rich productiveness was inspired by "the spirit of Newman"; "Newman and the Second Spring of Hopkins' Poetry," *The Hopkins Quarterly* VI, no. 3 (1974) 119-38.

/65/*Poems*, p. 78.

/66/*Poems*, p. 81.

/67/*Poems*, p. 82.

/68/*Poems*, p. 79.

/69/*Poems*, p. 80.

/70/*Poems*, p. 84.

/71/*Papers*, p 81.

/72/*Papers*, p. 83.

/73/Devlin, pp. 338-42.

/74/Robinson, pp. 89–103.

/75/Robinson, p. 92.

/76/See Schneider, chapter 8, for a useful discussion of stylistic change in Hopkins' last poems.

/77/*Poems*, p. 69.

/78/*Papers*, p. 83.

/79/*Poems*, p. 90.

/80/*Poems*, pp. 89, 90.

/81/*Papers*, p. 221.

/82/*Poems*, p. 86.

/83/*Poems*, pp. 97–98, 91.

/84/See Devlin, pp. 213–19. See Harris, pp. 20–40, note 85.

/85/*Poems*, p. 98.

/86/*Poems*, p. 101.

/87/Donald Walhout, *Send My Roots Rain: A Study of Religious Experience in the Poetry of Gerard Manley Hopkins* (Athens: Ohio University Press, 1981), p. 7. After Walhout's book appeared, Daniel Harris published a book titled, *Inspirations Unbidden: The "Terrible Sonnets" of Gerard Manley Hopkins* (Berkeley: University of California Press, 1982). Harris put forth a realignment of Hopkins' last poems based upon his interpretation of the corrections Hopkins made on his manuscripts as well as their transcriptive placement in what are now known as folios 29–35. Harris' thesis is that perhaps Hopkins deliberately "masked" his personal despair because he did not want to acknowledge his dejected state to Robert Bridges who was generally unsympathetic to his religion and his vocation. The fact is, Harris argues, that the sequence of the last poems, while not definitive in every segment, is one which reveals a priest and a poet in major physical, mental, and spiritual degeneration. Harris also argues that the internal evidence of Hopkins' last editing of "To Seem the Stranger" strongly affirms that the final version was not "in its final state an early or middle poem in the 'terrible sonnets.' " Placement of this sonnet of alienation and despair to a later position in the sequence, together with other evidence, makes doubtful that these last poems portray "a triumphant exhibition of God's grace." (It is true that Walhout's book is based upon a sequencing of the poems suggesting a gradual spiritual equilibrium being regained by the poet.) Finally, Harris, unable to prove any distinct pattern within the sequence of these poems, describes them "as a mere group, in a contiguous but not patterned assemblage, one whose aspects must be elucidated within." Rachel Salmon suggests a rich critical alternative: "By thinking of the nature and terrible sonnets as representations of coterminous and coextensive aspects of the life of the spirit (disregarding, that is, the particular order of the composition), we can examine their structure synchronically. Instead of tracing a process of development in Hopkins' aesthetic and religious life, we can focus attention upon the way that the features of each sonnet cycle relate to those of the other." In *Victorian Poetry* 22 (1984) 389.

Norman MacKenzie writes in his *Reader's Guide to Gerard Manley Hopkins* (Ithaca: Cornell University Press, 1981), pp. 169-71: "There is, in fact, no agreed list of these 'Dark Sonnets,' or title which will cover with equal warrant more than a few of them. Even to arrange a central seven in a series of lessening discouragement is to invite challenge. . . . Nor should we imagine that their chronology can be settled by regarding them as a brightening sequence from the midnight of despair to the relief of a dawn survivor —nor, as some would prefer, the reverse. This is as alluring and inconclusive a pastime as the renumbering of Shakespeare's sonnets." MacKenzie is surely right. The issue of the sequence of these last poems of Hopkins will never be settled. Harris notwithstanding, there is no irrefutable argument for making the sequence of poems end in the abyss. Not one of these last poems is a declaration of final despair. Within every one of them is an overwhelming spiritual determination to reach out of the darkness to find the meaning of the Lord's mastery. These great sonnets are testimony of the sanctifying imagination operating at mysterious levels of elevated religious consciousness.

/88/*Poems,* p. 99.

/89/*Poems,* pp. 100, 101

/90/*Poems,* p. 102.

/91/*Poems,* p. 105.

/92/*Poems,* p. 106.

/93/*Poems,* pp. 106-8.

/94/See Walhout for a good discussion of the coherence of Hopkins' philosophy of religion, chapter 7, of which I have liberally made use.

/95/Bloom, p. xxv.

/96/*Poems,* p. 91.

INDEX OF TITLES AND FIRST LINES
OF WORKS CITED

Andromeda, 71

As kingfishers catch fire, dragonflies draw flame, 58–60, 61, 79–80

Binsey Poplars, 55–56, 69–70

Bugler's First Communion, The, 70

Candle Indoors, The, 70

Carrion Comfort, 91–93, 95–96

Duns Scotus' Oxford, 71

Escorial, The, 13–14

Felix Randall, 80–81

God's Grandeur, 38, 60–61

Habit of Perfection, The, 14

Handsome Heart, The, 70

Henry Purcell, 71

Hurrahing in Harvest, 61

I wake and feel the fell of dark, not day, 94, 95–96, 97–99

In the Valley of the Elwy, 61

Inversnaid, 55–56, 80

Lantern out of Doors, The, 61

Loss of Eurydice, The, 67

Leaden Echo and the Golden Echo, The, 61, 81, 115

May Magnificat, The, 67

My own heart let me more have pity on; let, 99–102

No worst, there is none. Pitched past pitch of grief, 93–94, 95–96

Origin of Our Moral Ideas, The (essay), 72–73, 76

Patience, 99–102

Penmaen Pool, 55–56

Peace, 71

Pied Beauty, 61, 77–78

Probable Future of Metaphysics, The (essay), 17

Ribblesdale, 55–56, 80

St. Alphonsus Rodriguez, 104

The shepherd's brow, fronting
  forked lightning, owns, 105

Spelt from Sibyl's Leaves, 81

Spring, 61

Spring and Fall, 70

Starlight Night, The, 61

That Nature is a Heraclitean
  Fire and of the comfort of
  the Resurrection, 102-4

Thou art indeed just, Lord, if I
  contend, 104-5

To R. B., 105-7

To seem the stranger seems
  my lot, my life, 86-87, 124
  n.87

To What Serves Mortal
  Beauty?, 81, 83-85

Windhover, The, 31, 33-34,
  61-67, 76

Wreck of the Deutschland,
  The, 2, 12, 38, 41-42, 45-54,
  55, 60, 64, 66, 69, 91, 122
  n.55

INDEX OF PROPER NAMES

Abrams, M. H., 57

Alphonsus, Saint, 104

Augustine, Saint, 9, 57, 85

Blake, William, 3, 27, 47, 52, 57, 61, 66, 108

Bloom, Harold, 3, 13; *The Visionary Company*, 113-14

Bridges, Robert, 46-47, 114, 117 n.1, 123-24 n.87

Byron, George Gordon, 57

Calvin, Calvinism, 81-82

Coleridge, S. T., 3, 4-5, 6-7, 8, 9, 10-12, 13, 22, 23, 27, 28, 31, 36, 39, 52, 57, 106, 108, 114, 116-17 n.1, 119 n.29, 120 n.3; *Rime of the Ancient Mariner*, 12, 57

Dante, *Divine Comedy*, 60

Devlin, Fr. C., 24, 82, 119-20 n.30

Dixon, R. W., 116 n.1, 117 n.1

Dorothea, Saint, 41

Frye, Northrop, 52

Gregory, Pope, 85

Harris, Daniel, 75, 82, 96, 123-24 n.87

Hegel, Hegelian, 81

Ignatius, Saint, Ignatian, 23, 25-27, 28-31, 31-34, 36, 37 38, 39, 42, 57-58, 58-60, 76 77, 79, 81, 97-99, 110, 120 n.30; *The Spiritual Exercises*, 24, 25-27, 28-31 33, 37, 59-60, 87, 119-20 n.30

John, Saint, 51, 122 n.55

Keats, John, 3, 27, 57, 117 n.

Kingsley, Charles, 8, 44

Leavis, F. R., 53

MacKenzie, Norman, 54, 124 n.87

Mary, Saint, 51

Miller, J. H., 96

Milton, John, 13, 57, 92; *Paradise Lost*, 60

Newman, Cardinal John Henry, 2, 3, 7-11, 12, 16, 23, 24-25, 44, 114, 117 n.10, 120 n.30, 122 n.64; *A Grammar of Assent*, 9-10, 24; *Apologia Pro Vita Sua*, 8

Parmenides, 43, 62, 77

Patmore, Coventry, 116-17 n.1

Paul, Saint, 9, 84

Pater, Walter, 31, 42-43, 44, 62-63, 72-73, 76, 81, 83, 84-85; *Marius the Epicurean*, 43

Plato, Platonic, 3, 16-17, 18, 40, 43

Prickett, Stephen, 3, 5, 6, 10-11

Rahner, Karl, 57

Read, Herbert, 96

Richards, I. A., 96

Robinson, John, 14, 31-33, 43, 51, 52-53, 75-76, 89

Ruskin, John, 63, 109

Salmon, Rachel, 124 n.87

Schneider, Elisabeth, 14, 31, 51

Scotus, John Duns, Scotian, 2, 22, 23, 24, 25, 31, 35, 36-39, 42, 55, 58, 59-60, 66, 74, 76, 77, 79, 97-99, 119 n.30, 120 n.31

Shakespeare, William, 16

Shea, F. X., 13

Shelley, Percy Bysshe, 27, 57

Spenser, Edmund, 57

Stevens, Wallace, 13

Suarez, Francisco, 22, 35, 77

Walhout, Donald, 88-89, 105, 123 n.87, 124 n.87

Wordsworth, William, 3, 4, 6, 7-8, 10, 11, 13, 16, 27, 31, 38, 57, 61, 93, 108, 116-17 n.1, 120 n.30; "Immortality" ode, 4, 21, 56; *The Prelude*, 4

Yeats, W. B., 13, 26, 61